THE TASTES OF HOME

ABOUT THE AUTHOR

Dr Ong Jin Teong was born and raised in a Penang Nonya family and was encouraged by his mother to cook at an early age. A retired professor of Electrical Engineering, he has extensively researched Penang and Nonya cuisines and is a sought-after authority on the subjects. He is the author of *Penang Heritage Food: Yesterday's Recipes for Today's Cook* which won the best culinary history national award and *Nonya Heritage Kitchen, Origins, Utensils and Recipes* which was hailed best in the world for culinary history, both in the Gourmand World Cookbook Awards.

Text: copyright © 2024 Ong Jin Teong
Photographs: copyright © 2024 Landmark Books Pte Ltd

Cover graphics: Lim Huiling
Interior graphics: Lim Anling

All rights reserved. No part of this publication may be reproduced or transmitted in any format by any means, electronic or mechanical, including photocopy, recording or any information storage and retrieval system, without prior permission in writing from the publisher.

Published by
Landmark Books Pte Ltd

ISBN 978-981-18-9672-9

Printed by KHL Printing Co Pte Ltd

THE TASTES OF HOME

Easy-to-Cook Dishes from Singapore & Malaysia

ONG Jin Teong

·LANDMΔRK·BOOKS·

Contents

Introduction 7

The Basics 9

Eggs 27

Rice & Porridge 41

Noodles 61

Main Dishes 87

Desserts 157

Index 170

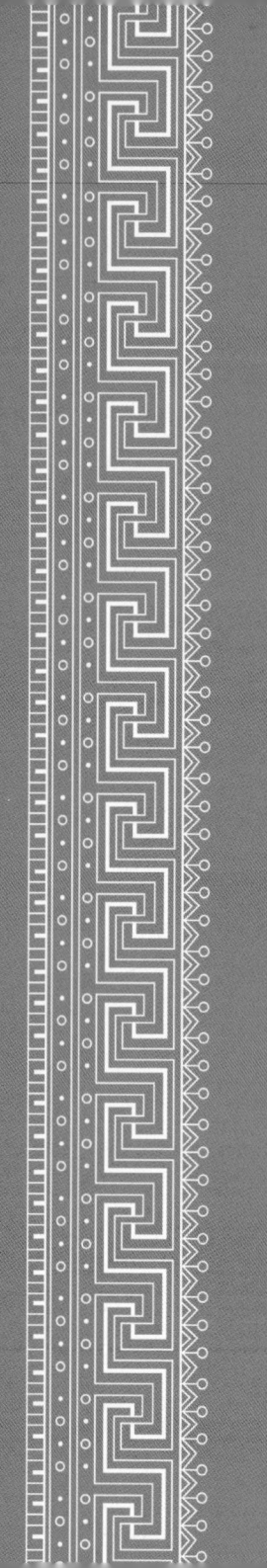

Introduction

The purpose of this book is to help people who have little experience in cooking or would like to learn to cook homely food from Singapore and Malaysia. It is especially useful to students leaving home for further studies and those, including newly-weds, setting up home. I hope that readers will progress from basic to more elaborate cooking. Hence, I have added some advanced options that, if adopted, will increase the variety of dishes in your repertoire.

This book has chapters on dishes using eggs, rice and noodles as the main ingredient, followed by two other chapters on main courses, and desserts.

I start with simple dishes that I cooked as an undergraduate in London many years ago. I then recall the easy-to-cook dishes prepared by my mother and the food I grew up with in Penang. As these are uncomplicated dishes, the recipes were not commonly recorded in writing until now.

My research was helped by my cousin Siew Yoong's desire to document the everyday dishes cooked by her mother and her sister Sandy who prepared numerous dishes whenever I was in Kuala Lumpur. Sandy was also very generous with her help in explaining how these dishes were cooked.

I find it interesting that many of my Penang family's easy-to-cook dishes have their counter-parts in Singapore and Melaka.

So, I know that as you use the recipes in this book, you will create the foods that bring you the comforting tastes of home.

1: THE BASICS

WEIGHTS AND MEASURES

There is no agreed international standard for measuring cups or spoons. The British and the American cups are not the same and, to add to the confusion, there are breakfast cups, tea cups and coffee cups!

The cup used in this book has a capacity of 240 ml which is close enough to most national standards.

As for the volumes of a teaspoon and tablespoon, there is a near international consensus except for the Australians. In this book a teaspoon has a capacity of 5 ml and a tablespoon, 15 ml.

A digital weighing scale is highly recommended for your kitchen. It is worth noting that one millilitre (ml) of water weighs 1 gram so a weighing scale can be conveniently used to measure the volume of water. In other words, the weight of water in grams and the volume in millilitres are interchangeable.

As a rough guide, 10 ml of oil weighs about 9 g – about 10 percent less than water since oil has a lower density compared to water.

SAFE FOOD HANDLING

It is extremely important to cultivate and adhere to safe food handling practices as the effects of food poisoning are very serious and unpleasant.

Wash your hands before cooking.

When the room temperature is high, cooked food to be kept overnight should be heated up, kept covered to cool, and stored in a closed container in the refrigerator.

A pot of soup too big for a refrigerator is cooked and not disturbed; the cover should not be opened till the soup is ready to be heated up before serving. This is to prevent contaminating the soup.

Cooked and raw food should not be mixed. Raw vegetables should be kept separate from other raw food especially in the refrigerator. Ideally, separate chopping boards should be used for raw meat and vegetables to prevent cross-contamination by pathogenic bacteria. If the same chopping board and knife are used, process the vegetable or cooked meat, and then thoroughly clean the chopping board and knife, preferably with hot water, before preparing the other type of ingredient. Then wash the chopping board, the knife and your hands.

Frozen meat should be thoroughly thawed before cooking, especially chicken. Transfer from the freezer to the fridge to thaw or use a microwave oven. Frozen fish doesn't have to be fully thawed before cooking.

When using a microwave oven for warming cooked food, do ensure that the food is hot enough to kill pathogen bacteria. Bacteria thrive in temperatures up to about 60°C but will not survive above about 74°C, so, to be safe, heat cooked or leftover food to about 80°C.

Leftover cooked rice should be kept in the refrigerator. When cooked rice is left at room temperature in the tropics or in the summer in temperate climate, the *bacillus cereus* spores grow into bacteria which will cause food poisoning,

Towels, cloths and sponges used for cleaning worktops, dishes and kitchen utensils should be washed with hot water regularly. Dishwashing sponges should be similarly washed, then rinsed and squeezed dry.

UTENSILS

When I was a student in London in the Sixties and early Seventies, my only cooking vessel was an army mess tin from my scouting days in Penang. I didn't have a cover for it until I made one in the university workshop in my postgraduate days.

Rice cookers were not so common in those days, so I didn't own one. It would have been very useful.

In the next section, I have made a list of basic cooking utensils you will need to start off your culinary journey, together with another optional list. If you can afford it, buy high-quality utensils which will last a lifetime. If you are a student, you may be able to inherit utensils from your seniors who are graduating. Or you can do both!

Basic Utensils
- Rice cooker, preferably one with steamer attachment. A basic rice cooker is easier to clean.
- Frying pan, preferably a wok
- Frying ladle
- Saucepan of about 1.5- to 2-litre capacity. Saucepans have tall, straight sides and a single handle. They typically come with a lid. Saucepans are smaller than stock pots and Dutch ovens which have two handles and are deeper than saucepans.
- Weighing scale
- Chopper. If you can handle the weight, get a heavier one
- Small knife
- Knife sharpener or sharpening stone
- A chopping board or boards
- Colander with an accompanying container
- Can opener
- Potato and vegetable peeler
- Hand-held grater (similar to potato and vegetable peeler)
- Small ladle
- Wooden spoon
- Basic crockery: Chinese rice bowls, dinner plates, side plates, sauce plates, serving plates and bowls, serving bowl for soup
- Basic cutlery: knives, forks, spoons, teaspoons, Chinese soup spoons, chopsticks.

Optional Utensils
- Round, flat steaming tray
- Mandoline for slicing or julieinne cuts.
- A wire sieve or wire basket for deep-frying.
- Plastic spatula

INGREDIENTS

I have made a list of basic ingredients that you will need to prepare your own meals. Most of the ingredients, like dried prawns, dried mushroom and a variety of dried noodles, have a fairly long shelf life. You can buy the optional ingredients when you need them.

Basic Ingredients
- Rice
- Dried noodles – *bee hoon*, *koay teow*, *tung hoon*, egg noodles, *mee sua* (see pages 60-62)
- Eggs
- Dried mushrooms
- Dried prawns
- Flour
- Cooking oil
- Ginger
- Shallots
- Onions
- Garlic
- Potatoes
- Sugar
- Salt
- White pepper
- Black pepper
- Light soya sauce
- Dark soya sauce
- Tomato sauce
- Chilli sauce
- Corn flour or corn starch
- Chicken or vegetable stock cubes

Optional Ingredients
- Vinegar
- Sesame oil
- Chilli powder
- Coriander powder
- Ngoh Hiang Hoon (5-spice powder)
- Tamarind
- Tamarind slices (*assam gelugor*)
- Cloves
- Cinnamon
- Cumin (*jintan puteh*)
- Fennel (*jintan manis*)
- Salted fermented soya beans (*tau cheo*)
- Black beans
- Shrimp paste (*belacan*). The powdered form is convenient
- Sesame seeds

CUTTING AND SLICING TECHNIQUES

Traditionally, ingredients are cut more finely by the Nonyas or Straits Chinese, especially in Penang, probably following the customary Hokkien practice. Slicing and cutting by Cantonese home cooks are less fine.

Today, various gadgets like a mandoline – spelt with an 'e' at the end – and various types of graters can be used for cutting. However, it is good to acquire the basic skills of using a knife or small chopper to cut and slice. A mandoline is useful for slicing and grating a large quantity of vegetable as when preparing the filling for Poh Piah or Spring Rolls. For small quantities, it is not worth the effort of washing the parts after use!

A simple hand-held vegetable shredder or peeler is convenient for shredding small quantities of root vegetable like carrots and potatoes. There are also multifunction vegetable peelers and slicers.

Cutting with a Knife or Chopper

Grip the handle of the knife with your dominant hand. You could rest your index finger on top of the

blunt side of the blade near the handle. Place the tip of the knife on the chopping board. The tip should be more or less in the same position when cutting. If you are cutting a lot of ingredients, it may be more convenient to lift the knife higher so that the tip of the knife can move forward. You will have to do that for cutting meat.

If you are right-handed, place the vegetables to be cut on the left side of the knife and hold the vegetables down with your thumb and forefinger. If it is a pile or several pieces, hold the vegetables with the other fingers too. The guiding finger or thumb is the one closer to the blade of the knife and positioned highest on the vegetables. The cutting is done by lifting the handle-end of the blade to just below the level of the guiding finger so that when the blade is moved down to slice, the finger or thumb is unlikely to be accidentally cut by the knife. For slicing vegetables, the movement of the knife is downwards with slight movement forward when the handle end of the blade touches the chopping board. For cutting meat, the forward movement of the blade has to be more accentuated.

Vegetables, especially root vegetables, are cut in a variety of ways for different dishes.

Cutting Carrots

If carrots are fresh and clean, they don't need to be peeled. Otherwise, use a peeler to remove the skin. Slice off the top and tip of each carrot.

To cut rings, slice the carrot crosswise to about 2-3 mm in thickness. For elliptical slices, cut at a slant across its length.

To julienne or cut into strips, slice thinly at a slant across the length of the carrot. Then gather the slices together and cut finely into strips.

To dice, first cut a carrot into barrels of about 5-cm long, then cut each in half lengthwise. Rest the cut carrot on its flat edge and slice into 5-mm sticks. Arrange the sticks together in a pile and cut into small cubes.

Clockwise from top left: chunks, sticks, strips, elliptical slices, rings, cubes.

To cut into chunks, cut the carrot into barrels of convenient lengths then slice each barrel in half, lengthwise if the carrot is thin. If the carrots are fatter, cut each half into 3 or 4 segments lengthwise. Gather all the lengths and cut into chunks of about 2 to 3 cm.

Cutting Potatoes

Use a peeler to remove the potato skin.

For potato chips, cut the potatoes into slices according to your preferred thickness.

For potato sticks, cut the potatoes as for chips to

Clockwise from top: slices, cubes and sticks.

1 cm thickness, then stack the slices and cut into sticks.

For diced potatoes, prepare potato sticks, gather them and cut into small cubes. Adjust the thickness of your slices according to your preferred cube size. The recipes in this book call for half-cm cubes.

Cutting Onions

Peel and discard the onion skin.

To cut into rings, hold the onion with the root end facing the blade of the knife. Cut off and discard the root end and tip. Cut the onion into rings of a minimum of

4 mm thickness or your preferred thickness.

For slices, cut the onion into half from shoot to root. Cut a v-shape to remove the root of each half of the onion. Lay each half of the onion with the shoot end facing the blade of the knife and cut into slices of your preferred thinness.

To cut onions into wedges, first slice them into two from shoot to root. Cut a v-shape to remove the root of each half of the onion. Cut each half of the onion into six equal wedges.

To dice, turn the wedges by 90 degrees and cut them into 4 or 5 equal parts.

From top: rings, slices, wedges and dice.

Cutting Garlic

The most convenient way of peeling garlic is to first smash the cloves using the side of a chopper. This makes it is easier to remove the skin. I normally cut off the root end of the garlic.

Arrange the peeled garlic cloves together lengthwise and cut into strips, then turn the strips by 90 degrees and chop into bits. If the garlic is not fine enough, chop randomly till you get the fineness you wish.

Chopped garlic is fried in oil and used as garnishing. It is a commonly used to cook seafood, especially prawn dishes.

Anti-clockwise from top right: chopped garlic, smashed garlic, sliced garlic, halved shallot, sliced shallot, shallot rings.

Cutting Shallots

Peel and discard the skin of the shallots.

To cut into rings, hold the shallot with the root end facing the knife blade. Cut off and discard the root end and tip. Cut the shallot into rings of about 1 mm thick. Shallot rings are normally fried for use as garnishing.

For slices, cut the shallot into half from shoot to root. Cut a v-shape to remove the root of each half of the shallots. Lay each half of the shallot with the shoot end facing the blade of the knife and cut into slices of about 1-mm thickness. Shallots are cut this way for Nasi Ulam. Use your thumbs and index fingers to break up the slices for eating raw.

Cutting Cabbage

Some people don't like cabbage because, if it is not well cooked, it has a slightly bitter taste. Thus, it is important to slice cabbage properly so that it can be cooked through.

I prefer to use the slightly green cabbage rather than the white ones which have thicker leaves.

Cut off and set aside the thick centre stalk of each leaf of cabbage. Stack the leaves and slice thinly into 2-4 mm strips according to your preference. Slice the stalks finely and cook them with the sliced leaves.

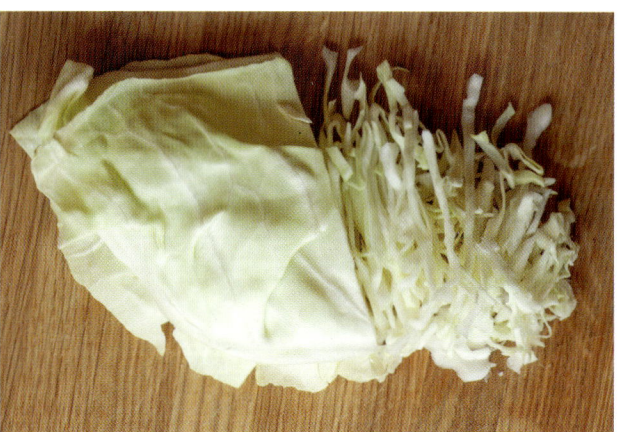

Sliced cabbage.

Cutting Mushrooms

Fresh or canned mushrooms are used in Hainanese Western-influenced dishes. For Chicken Pie or stew, the mushrooms are cut into wedges while they are diced for Min Chee, and Mushroom and Tung Hoon Soup. Slice or wedge mushrooms for Chinese and noodle dishes.

To slice mushrooms, cut off the stems if they are too long so that the mushroom caps can sit well on the chopping board. Cut the caps into 5 mm slices or to your preferred thickness.

To cut mushrooms into wedges, cut off the stalk and hold the cap firmly on the chopping board. Cut in half, then cut each half into two. For larger mushrooms cut each half into three pieces.

To dice mushrooms, cut off the stalk and slice the cap into two horizontally. Keep the two parts stacked on top of one another and cut into 1-cm strips. Collect the strips and turn them by 90 degrees and cut to dice.

Do not throw away the mushroom stalks. They can be cooked with the rest of the mushrooms. Cut them into thin slices of about 2 mm.

Cutting Cucumber

There is really no need to remove the skin from cucumbers. They are more crunchy when served with

From left: sliced mushrooms, diced mushrooms and mushroom wedges.

the skin. Traditionally, we cut off an inch or so of both ends of the cucumber, and use these pieces to rub on the cut part of the cucumber to draw out the bitter sap. Once that is done, cut off a slice of ½ cm on either end, and the cucumber is ready to be used.

These days, cucumber that is bitter is less common and cucumber with dark green skin, which are not bitter at all, are available.

To slice a cucumber, start by cutting off both ends and draw out the bitter sap as described above, if required. Now cut the cucumber into thin slices of about 3 mm or to your preferred thickness. Sliced cucumber is put in egg sandwiches.

To julienne or cut cucumber into strips, first cut it into slices as described above. Stack a few slices and cut into strips of equal thickness according to your preference. Julienne cucumber is one of the garnishes for Assam Laksa and Lemak Laksa.

Cucumber wedges are used in fruit rojak and as an accompaniment for Satay and Nasi Lemak. You cut cucumber into wedges on a chopping board by rotating it by a third of its circumference after each cut. Alternatively, cut it like the rojak seller by holding the cucumber in one hand and cutting small wedges off the cucumber as you rotate it.

Cucumbers used in Acar Awak and cooked in a sweet and sour sauce are normally cut into pieces with the core removed. First cut the cucumbers into quarters, lengthwise. Remove the core and cut the quarters into lengths according to your preference. For fatter cucumbers you may want to cut them into eighths instead of quarters.

Cutting Broccoli
The florets are the clusters of flowers of the broccoli, while the spears are the stalks. Both can be eaten. Cut off about 5 cm from the bottom of the stalk. Peel off the thick, fibrous skin with a knife and slice the stalks

until you reach the florets. For stir frying, each floret should be cut into 2 to 4 pieces.

Cutting Cauliflower
Cauliflower is cut in the same way as broccoli.

Cutting Chai Sim (Chinese Flowering Cabbage)
Chai sim from Malaysia normally has leaf stalks longer than the leaves and hardly any stem. Hong Kong *chai sim*, which is known in Cantonese as *choy sum*, has thick stems with leaves and leaf stalks.

For Malaysian *chai sim*, the bottom 1 cm is cut off and discarded. Separate the leaves from the stalks and cut them into 3-cm pieces.

For Hong Kong *choy sum*, cut off the stems and slice them at a slant. Cut the leaves and leaf stalks into two or three parts.

Stringing Beans
Beans, especially the more mature ones, should be strung to remove the fibrous edges. To string a bean, hold the stem with your thumb and forefinger and give it a twist till the stem breaks but is still connected to the pod. Pull the stem along the edge of the bean to remove the fibre.

Cutting Meat
Use a sharp knife to cut meat. The blade should be moved downwards and, as it nears the chopping board, pushed forward.

Buy a whole slab rather than thick slices of belly pork. To cut into strips, first cut the belly pork into slices of about 2-3 mm thickness. Stack the slices together and cut into strips of about 2-3 mm.

For dishes that require belly pork to be cut into strips, I suggest that you first boil the meat till it is cooked. This is because cooked meat is firmer and becomes much easier to cut.

FRYING

Frying Garlic or Shallots

Heat up a pan or wok. Place your hand over the wok to check the heat. When it is hot – you should feel the heat when you place your palm over the pan – add the oil and, when hot again, add the sliced shallots or chopped garlic. Stir continuously to prevent burning.

Turn off the heat when the garlic or shallots just turn golden. They will continue cooking till golden brown in the residual heat.

Move the fried garlic or shallots to the edge of the wok. Drain the oil, then transfer the fried garlic or shallots to a saucer. These days, you can buy fried garlic and shallots.

Stir Frying

When stir-frying, you start by frying the chopped garlic or sliced shallot. In general, garlic is used with seafood while sliced shallots are for meat.

Vegetable stems, which take longer to cook, are added first. Mushrooms are included early on to absorb the flavours. Then meat or seafood is added.

Salt or light soya sauce is put in next. The leaves of vegetables, especially the finely sliced ones, and peas and beans, are the last to go in.

Shallow frying

The wok should be first heated up and, when hot, enough oil is poured in to be able to partially cover the items to be fried.

Items being fried should be turned so that every piece is uniformly fried. The fried items are removed from the oil when golden brown. A wire colander is useful to drain the oil.

PREPARING SPICE PASTE (*REMPAH*) FOR CURRY

For beginners, it is more convenient to use commercially prepared curry pastes to cook curry. There are several companies that produce all types of curry paste. You only need to add meat and coconut milk to these pastes.

The more difficult alternative is to use commercially prepared curry powder. First, mix the curry powder with water to make a paste (*rempah*). Next, heat oil in a pan to fry chopped onions till they become transparent. Lastly, add the curry paste to *tumis* (fry) till fragrant and the oil separates from the *rempah*. This process is rather time-consuming if cooking large quantities.

BEFORE YOU START COOKING
Read the recipe carefully before you start cooking.

Get all the cooking utensils and ingredients that are required ready. *Mise en place* is the French term for having the ingredients washed, weighed, sliced, grated or chopped before you start cooking. Group your ingredients in the order of use according to the recipe.

Wash up and clean-up as you cook!

2: EGGS

Eggs are widely available, have a long shelf life and are hence a useful ingredient for easy-to-cook meals. They can be soft-boiled, hard-boiled, scrambled, fried and put in many simple dishes.

Soft-boiled and hard-boiled-eggs can be taken by themselves with bread or included in a range of dishes. You can make egg sandwiches with hard-boiled eggs.

Eggs can be beaten and fried with a variety of ingredients like onions, mushrooms and chillies for a variety of omelettes.

For the more adventurous, try preparing Fu Yong Hai, the poor man's "shark fins" fried with egg that uses *tung hoon* (glass noodles) instead of shark fins. (*See* page 38.)

The scrambled eggs known as Aw Aw Nui on page 32 is our Ong family heirloom recipe handed down by my paternal grandmother.

All dishes in this chapter are prepared using two eggs.

Soft-boiled Eggs

This is the style of eggs served in kopitiam *(coffee shops) in Singapore and Malaysia. It is important to start with eggs that are at room temperature. If the temperature of the eggs is too cold, there is a higher risk of the egg cracking when put into boiling water. Cold eggs will also take longer to cook. The method given here is for medium-sized eggs (about 55 g).*

Pour in 750 ml of water into a saucepan and put in two eggs. Add a little more water if the water does not cover the eggs. Remove the eggs and boil the water. Turn off the heat when it has come to a boil. Carefully put the eggs back into the saucepan; do not drop them!

Do not cover the saucepan. After 5½ minutes, remove the eggs from the hot water. Transfer the eggs to a bowl of room temperature water to stop the cooking process. Adjust the timing if you prefer firmer egg yolk, or are using larger or smaller eggs.

Crack the eggs into a bowl. Scrape the egg white from the egg shells. Serve with soya sauce, ground pepper and toast.

Hard-boiled Eggs

For hard-boiled eggs, follow the method for soft-boiled eggs but increase the water to 1 litre and the cooking time to 12 minutes. The yolk will be firm. The timing is a rough guide and depends on how hard you like the yolks to be. If you like the yolks a bit harder, add another 1 or 2 minutes to the cooking time.

Drain the water and fill the saucepan with cold water. Crack the shells all over and remove the shells and the membrane which cover the eggs. It is best to remove the shells before the eggs become cold, otherwise it will be more difficult to shell the eggs.

Serve with light soya sauce or Worcestershire sauce.

Egg Sandwich

2 hard-boiled eggs
1 tsp butter
1 tsp light soya sauce
1 tsp Worcestershire sauce
Pepper to taste
4 slices of bread
Sliced cucumber, optional
Sliced tomato, optional
Lettuce, optional

Cut the hard-boiled egg into slices of about ½ cm thick. Use an egg slicer if you have one. Put the slices of egg into a bowl and add the butter. The butter will melt quickly if the eggs are still warm. Use a knife to cut the egg into smaller pieces, mixing in the butter. Add the light soya and Worcestershire sauces and mix thoroughly. Sprinkle or grind some pepper over the egg.

If you wish, spread some butter on a slice of bread. Spoon on the prepared hard-boiled egg. For a balanced meal, you could add sliced cucumber or tomato or lettuce to your sandwich. Cover with a second piece of bread. Do the same for the other two slices of bread. For an elegant presentation, slice each sandwich into four triangular pieces.

Aw Aw Nui
HEIRLOOM SCRAMBLED EGGS

This is a simple heirloom egg dish that came through my paternal grandmother. The eggs should be scrambled but not overcooked. The whites should be cooked till they turn from transparent to brilliant white and remains soft.

2 eggs
1 tsp black soya sauce
1 tsp light soya sauce
½ tsp sesame oil, optional
Pepper, to taste
2 slices of bread, optional
2 tsp oil
4 small shallots, peeled and sliced thinly

Break the eggs into a bowl. Add 2 half egg shells of water, the black and light soya sauces and sesame oil, if using. Grind or sprinkle pepper over the egg. If you wish to serve the scrambled eggs on toast, toast the bread.

Heat up a frying pan. When it is hot – you should feel the heat when you place your palm over the pan – spread the oil uniformly on the pan.

Add the sliced shallot and spread them out on the pan. Just as the shallots turn transparent, pour the eggs in and scramble. Be prepared to remove the scrambled eggs onto a plate or onto slices of toast as soon as the egg whites turn from transparent to white.

OMELETTES

An omelette can be served as a simple meal on its own or with bread as a sandwich or with rolls. It can also be served with other dishes in a meal.

Onions go well with eggs. Other common ingredients used in Southeast Asia for omelettes are *lap cheong* (Chinese sausage, *see* page 36), chillies and *char siew* (grilled pork). Mushrooms, grated cheese, chopped-up ham or bacon can also be used.

The eggs should be beaten up with half an egg shell of water to every egg used. Additional ingredients should be sliced – Chinese sausage and chillies should be cut into 2- or 3-mm slices, and *char siew* cut into slices and then into strips

Lap Cheong Omelette

2 eggs
1 tsp light soya sauce
Ground pepper
1 small onion, about 30 g
2 tsp oil
Sliced red chillies, optional
Chinese sausage *(lap cheong)*, sliced

Break the eggs into a bowl and add 2 half egg shells of water and the light soya sauce. Beat with a fork till the white and the yolks are well mixed but not foamy. Season with pepper.

Peel the onion and slice it into two from the shoot to the roots. Lay the halves flat on a chopping board and cut into slices about 3 mm thick.

Heat up a frying pan. When you can feel the heat when you place your palm above the pan, add 1 teaspoon of oil and spread it all over the pan. Then add the sliced onions, chillies, if using, and the sliced *lap cheong*. Spread the ingredients uniformly on the pan. When the onions start to become transparent, pour the eggs over evenly. Ensure that the sliced onions, chillies and the egg are uniformly distributed.

Wait for the omelette to cook on one side. Then use a ladle to cut the omelette into two. Drizzle another teaspoon of oil all over the omelette and turn each half of the omelette over. Cook for about a minute and lift the edge of the pieces with the ladle to see if they are ready. The omelette should soft inside and not crispy on the outside.

Other Omelettes
Try preparing omelettes with other fillings like mushrooms, ham, *char siew*, bacon or cheese.

Mushrooms, ham, bacon and *char siew* should be sliced.

Bacon should be fried first before the onions.

Cheese should be grated and added with the eggs.

When you have mastered making omelette, try cooking Fu Yong Hai (page 38).

Fu Yong Hai
EGG & FAUX SHARK FIN

This is a sustainable version of a dish served in Chinese banquets originally using eggs and shark fins. Since it is not right to eat shark fins, tung hoon (glass noodles) is used instead in this recipe. Only a small amount of tung hoon should be used, otherwise the dish will become fried tung hoon! Similarly, if too much egg is used, the dish will be an omelette!

Bamboo shoots and crabmeat are traditionally included. Canned crabmeat is a convenient choice.

2 eggs
10 g *tung hoon* (glass noodles), pre-soaked in warm water
1 tsp light soya sauce
Pepper, to taste
1 small onion, about 50 g
1 small carrot, about 50 g
3 sprigs spring onions
2 tsps oil
3 dried mushrooms, soaked and thinly sliced
50 g bamboo shoots cut into short, thin strips, optional
50 g ham, sliced and cut into 1-cm squares
50 g canned crabmeat, optional
Lettuce leaves

Break the eggs into a bowl and add the light soya sauce and pepper. Beat with a fork till the white and the yolks are well mixed but not foamy.

Peel the onion and slice it into two from the shoot to the roots. Lay the halves flat on a chopping board and cut into slices about 2-mm thick.

Cut the carrots into short, thin strips.

Cut the spring onions into lengths of about 3 cm.

Heat up the frying pan. When you can feel the heat when you place your palm above the pan, add 2 teaspoon of oil. Spread it all over the pan. Then add the sliced mushrooms, onions, carrots and bamboo shoots, if using.

Stir till the onions are slightly transparent. Then add the ham, *tung hoon* and

the crabmeat, if using. Stir to mix the ingredients.

Pour in the beaten eggs and mix well. Stop stirring and wait for the egg mixture to partially cook. Use the ladle to lift the edge of the egg to check if it is cooked and solidified. When done, give the mixture a good stir. Leave for about ½ minute, then give the Fu Yong Hai another stir. When the egg is cooked, give it a final stir.

Serve on the lettuce leaves.

3: RICE & PORRIDGE

Rice is the staple for the people of South and Southeast Asia, where the climate is suitable for rice cultivation. Koreans and Japanese also eat rice but of the short-grain variety. The rice used by the Italians for risotto and the Spaniards for paella are also short grain.

Rice is normally cooked by boiling or steaming. It is accompanied by meat, vegetable and other dishes. Fried rice is an easy-to-cook one-dish meal that is best prepared with leftover rice. Freshly cooked rice is not so good for fried rice because it is moist and sticky. If newly cooked rice is to be used, it should be left to cool before frying.

Rice porridge can be cooked using leftover rice or cooked from scratch. Either way, it takes more time to cook than rice. It is therefore best to plan ahead if you intend to cook porridge. Having a rice cooker or a slow cooker will make it more convenient.

In this chapter, the recipe for plain rice porridge feeds two. However, for flavoured porridge and fried rice, the portion is for one. The portions are scalable. So for two portions, double the quantity of the ingredients.

Cooking and Serving Rice
Measure the amount of rice required and put it into a pot or rice cooker. As a rough guide, about 70 g of white polished rice is sufficient for one person.

Wash the rice grains and drain away the water; repeat till the water is clear. Level the rice and add enough water to cover the rice by 1½ cm.

If you are cooking by weight, the amount of water needed is about twice the weight of the rice.

Keep in mind that the amount of water required depends on the type of rice being cooked. Jasmine rice commonly found in shops use the amount of water given above. Newly harvested rice needs less water and unpolished rice needs more water.

When cooked, rice should be gently stirred to separate the grains; rice should not be served in lumps.

If you prefer drier, more grainy rice which some prefer when eating with a curry, add enough water to cover the rice by 1¼ cm.

Cooking rice in a rice cooker

As it is best not to cook small amounts of rice in a rice cooker, cook at least two portions, that is 140 g of rice. Any excess rice can be kept for another meal. In warm climates, leftover rice must be stored in the refrigerator to keep it from going mouldy.

Make sure that the bottom of the rice cooker pot is dry. Wash the rice, drain the water, level the rice and add enough water to cover the rice by 1½ cm. Then turn the rice cooker on. When it switches off automatically, leave the rice to rest and cook fully for at least 10 minutes before serving.

Cooking rice in a pot

Wash 140 g of rice, drain the water and add enough water to cover the rice by 1½ cm. Bring the water to a boil. Cover the pot to keep the steam in and turn the heat to low to allow the rice to absorb the water for about 7 minutes. This will make enough rice for two portions.

Note that the rice may boil over and create a mess on the hob if the heat is not turned down in time. Turn off the heat and leave the rice to rest for at least 10 minutes before serving. The rice will continue cooking from the residual heat.

FRIED RICE

You can fry rice with a wide variety of ingredients. The basic ingredients, besides cooked rice, are oil, onion and egg. I like to include some vegetables and meat to make a nutritionally complete one-dish meal. For vegetables, you could use carrots, peas, beans, sweet corn, chopped celery and mushrooms. For convenience, frozen mixed vegetables can be used. For meat, you could use fresh or dried prawns, spam, ham or gammon, *char siew* or cooked meat like chicken, turkey, lamb and beef.

You may garnish with sliced lettuce, chillies, chopped spring onions and fried sliced onions.

The recipes for Cantonese Restaurant-style Fried Rice and a spicy Nonya Sambal Fried Rice are given in this chapter. You could make up your own versions of fried rice by using your favourite ingredients.

If the rice becomes too dry while it is being fried, you could add more oil or water to prevent it from sticking to the pan. I prefer to add one or two tablespoons of water.

Cantonese Restaurant-Style Fried Rice

1 Portion

180 g cooked rice
2 tsps oil
50 g onion, diced
50 g ham or cooked meat, chopped
50 g peas or mixed vegetables, thawed if frozen
1 tbsp light soya sauce
2 tbsps water
1 egg
2 sprigs spring onions, chopped finely
Lettuce, optional
Fried shallots, optional

Separate the grains of cooked rice with a fork or spoon.

Heat up a frying pan. When you can feel the heat when you place your palm above the pan, spread 1 teaspoon of the oil on the pan.

Add the diced onion and then the meat. Stir fry to heat up the meat.

Add the rice, vegetables, light soya sauce and the water. Give the fried rice a good stir. Fry for about 3 minute, stirring regularly; use your ladle to gently scrape the frying pan to ensure that the rice does not stick to the pan. If the rice sticks to the pan, add about 1 or 2 tablespoons of water and continue frying.

Move the fried rice to the edge of the pan. Add one teaspoon of oil and break the egg in the centre. Let it cook for about half a minute. Stir the egg to break it up, mixing it with the fried rice. Stir the fried rice thoroughly, then add the chopped spring onions and sliced lettuce, if using.

Your fried rice is ready to serve. You could top it with fried sliced shallots.

Nonya Sambal Fried Rice
1 Portion

This spicy Nonya fried rice is part of my early-childhood memories. It was a dish that my Aunty Rosie cooked when I attended the kindergarten next to her house on Clove Hall Road in Penang.

180 g cooked rice
2 tbsps dried prawn
1 onion, about 50 g
2 small red or green chillies, about 25 g
1 tsp ground toasted *belacan* (shrimp paste)
3 tsps oil
1 tbsp light soya sauce
1 egg
Fried sliced shallot, optional

Separate the grains of cooked rice with a fork or spoon.

Soak the dried prawns in 3 tablespoons of water. Strain and keep the water. Chop or pound the soaked dried prawns. Dice the onion and also the chillies.

If you have a mortar and pestle, pound the chopped dried prawns, the diced onion and diced chillies and ground *belacan* together.

Heat up a frying pan. When you can feel the heat when you place your palm above the pan, spread 2 teaspoons of the oil on the pan.

Add the dried prawns, onions, chillies and ground *belacan* (or the pounded ingredients). Fry the mixture till you get a strong, pungent smell.

Add the rice, light soya sauce and the water used to soak the dried prawns. Fry for about 3 minutes, stirring regularly; use your ladle to gently scrape the frying pan to separate the fried rice from the pan. If the rice sticks to the pan, add about 1 or 2 tablespoons of water and continue frying.

Move the fried rice to the edge of the pan, add one teaspoon of oil and break the egg in the centre. Let it cook for about half a minute then stir the egg to break it up, mixing it with the fried rice. Stir the fried rice thoroughly.

Serve your fried rice garnished with fried sliced shallots, if used.

RICE PORRIDGE

Rice porridge is often cooked from leftover rice. Water is added to the rice, which has been lightly stirred to separate the rice grains, before it is brought to the boil and then simmered.

A fast way of preparing rice porridge is to boil 140 g of flaked rice (*poha* or *aval*, available in Indian shops) with 650 ml of water in a pot or rice cooker. When it has boiled, give the rice a good stir. If using a rice cooker, switch-off and turn on the "keep-warm mode". If using a pot, simmer for about 10 minutes. This instant rice porridge is closer to Cantonese *chook* than Teochew *moi*.

If cooked rice is re-boiled with water for a short time, you get a grainy rice porridge. If the porridge is boiled for a longer time, a porridge with softer grains will result. If the porridge is boiled even longer, the rice grains will further soften and disintegrate. Different amounts of water are used to cook these different types of porridge preferred by different Chinese dialect groups.

Teochew porridge has rice grains which are slightly softer than cooked rice. Congee, also known as *chook* in Cantonese, is the result of simmering rice and water until the rice grains disintegrate. *Chook* turns into a thick gruel when it cools. The only way to thin the congee is to add water and re-boil it.

During and after the Second World War, due to the shortage of rice. sweet potato was added to bulk up rice porridge.

Traditionally, porridge is taken by those who are not

well or recuperating from illness because porridge is easier to digest.

You could eat Teochew *moi* or Cantonese *chook* with a selection of the following:

Boiled, fried or toasted peanuts
Boiled salted egg
Fried salt fish
Canned fish
Canned pickled vegetables
Omelette
Scrambled eggs

Cooking Teochew Moi in a Rice Cooker

2 Portions

Mix 360 g of leftover cooked rice with 400 ml of water in a rice cooker.

Switch on the rice cooker and switch if off after 15 minutes if it does not switch off automatically. The porridge may boil over, so lift the cover for a while if it does. If the rice cooker switches off before 15 minutes has passed, give the bottom of the pot a good stir and switch the rice cooker on again.

The porridge should be cooked for about 15 minutes in total. The cooking times are given as a guide depending on the rice cooker used. Add boiling water if you prefer your porridge thinner.

If cooked rice is not available, first cook rice as per normal. Wash 140 g raw rice in a rice cooker. Drain the water and add 280 ml of water to the rice. Switch on the rice cooker. When the rice cooker has switched off, add 400 ml of water and stir down to the bottom of the pot. Switch on the rice cooker again. This should yield about 380 g or about 2 bowls of Teochew *moi*. Add boiling water if you prefer your porridge thinner.

If you have a high-end rice cooker that has functions for cooking porridge, follow the instructions given in the manual. In general, you need more water to cook congee compared to Teochew *moi* and the cooking time is longer.

Cooking Teochew Moi without a Rice Cooker

2 Portions

Wash 140 g of raw rice and bring it to a boil with 680 ml of water. Stir the rice and then lower the heat to simmer for 15 minutes while leaving the pot slightly uncovered.

Cooking Cantonese Chook in a Rice Cooker

2 Portions

Wash 140 g of raw rice in a rice cooker and drain the water. Then add 280 ml of water to the rice. Switch on the rice cooker. Ten minutes after the rice cooker has switched off, add 280 ml of water, stir and switch on the rice cooker again. If cooked rice is used instead of raw rice, use 180 g instead of the newly cooked rice.

The rice cooker will take about 15 minutes to automatically switch off, depending on its capacity. When the rice cooker has automatically switched off, add 140 ml of water and stir down to the bottom of the pot. Switch on the rice cooker again and wait till the rice cooker automatically switches off.

When the rice cooker has automatically switched off, add another 140 ml of water and stir down to the bottom of the pot. Switch on the rice cooker again and wait till the rice cooker automatically switches off.

When the rice cooker has automatically switched off, add 280 ml of water and stir down to the bottom of the pot. Switch on the rice cooker again.

Leave the cover slightly uncovered so that the porridge will not boil over. Turn off the rice cooker after the porridge boils or after 15 minutes if it has not turned off automatically.

At this stage you have *chook*. If you like your *chook* thinner, add boiling water, stir and leave the rice cooker in the keep-warm mode.

Cooking Chook without a Rice Cooker

Wash 140 g of raw rice, drain the water and add enough water to cover the rice by 1½ cm. Bring the water to a boil. Cover the pot to keep the steam in and turn the heat to low to allow the rice to absorb the water for about 7 minutes.

After the rice is cooked, add 280 ml of water and stir to the bottom of the pot. Turn the heat to low and continue cooking for 10 minutes, stirring occasionally.

Add another 280 ml of water and stir to the bottom again. Cook for 10 minutes, stirring occasionally. Add boiling water and stir if you like thinner *chook*.

Minced Meat Rice Porridge
1 Portion

190 g or one rice bowl plain rice porridge
75 g minced meat, pork is traditionally used
2 stalks spring onions
1 tsp *tong chai* (preserved cabbage), optional
1 tsp sesame oil, optional
1 tsp cornflour
4 tsps light soya sauce
½ tsp salt
1 egg
Eu Char Koay (Chinese cruellers), optional
Pepper to taste

Chop the spring onions finely. Set aside half as garnish and keep the remainder to mix with the meatballs.

Coarsely chop up the *tong chai*, if using. Divide it into two equal portions, one for the meatballs and the other for cooking in the porridge.

Mix the minced meat with the sesame oil, if using, cornflour, 1 teaspoon of light soya sauce, the chopped spring onions, ground pepper and the chopped *tong chai*, if using. Use a teaspoon to fashion the minced pork mixture into balls of about 2 cm in diameter. Set aside.

Heat up the porridge in a saucepan and add the rest of the light soya sauce and the salt. Put in the meatballs when the porridge is boiling. Add a few tablespoon of water if the porridge becomes too thick. Stir till the meatballs are cooked; the colour will turn from pinkish to light brown. Add the other half of the *tong chai* and stir.

Turn off the heat and transfer the porridge into a serving bowl. Break an egg into the meatball porridge and stir till the egg is well mixed with the porridge.

The porridge is ready to be served. Garnish with the chopped spring onions and Eu Char Koay, if using, cut into bite-sized pieces. Season with pepper.

Fish Porridge
1 Portion

190 g or one rice bowl plain rice porridge
75 g fresh or frozen fish fillet
4 lettuce leaves or 2 stalks spring onions
Ginger, optional
¼ tsp salt
3 tsps light soya sauce
1 egg
Fried chopped garlic, optional
Eu Char Koay (Chinese cruellers), optional
1 tsp sesame oil, optional
Ground pepper to taste

Slice the lettuce leaves finely or chop the spring onions finely. Set aside as garnish.

If using ginger, scrape off the skin with the blunt side of a knife, then cut 2 slices of 1 - 2 mm thickness. Stack the slices and cut into thin strips.

If using frozen fish, put in the fridge or in water till it is almost completely thawed.

Cut the fish into slices about 1-cm thick, mix with the salt and set aside.

Heat up the porridge in a saucepan and add the light soya sauce. When the porridge is boiling, add the sliced fish and the sliced ginger, if using. Stir the porridge and turn off the heat as soon as the fish slices turn from transparent to white. This may take longer if the fish is partially frozen. It is best not to overcook the fish.

Transfer the porridge into a serving bowl. Break an egg into the fish porridge and stir till the egg is well mixed.

Garnish with the sliced lettuce or chopped spring onions, the fried chopped garlic and the Eu Char Koay cut into bite-sized pieces, if using. Add sesame oil and pepper as you prefer.

Chicken Porridge

1 Portion

190 g or one rice bowl plain rice porridge
75 g chicken
2 stalks spring onions
2 tsps light soya sauce
½ tsp salt
1 egg
Fried chopped garlic, optional
Eu Char Koay (Chinese cruellers), optional
Pepper to taste
1 tsp sesame oil, optional

Chop the spring onions finely. Set aside for garnishing.

Heat up the plain porridge in a saucepan. Put in the chicken and cook till it is cooked. Remove the chicken and turn off the heat. Shred the chicken and set aside.

Heat up the porridge again and add the light soya sauce and the salt. Stir in a few tablespoon of water if the porridge is too thick.

Turn off the heat and transfer the porridge into a serving bowl. Break an egg into the chicken porridge and stir till the egg is well mixed in. Spread the shredded chicken on the porridge.

Garnish with the chopped spring onions, fried chopped garlic and the Eu Char Koay cut into bite-sized pieces, if using. Add sesame oil and pepper as you prefer.

4: NOODLES

Noodles are readily available for preparing convenient one- or multi-course meals. There are many varieties of traditional Chinese noodles. Nowadays, there are also other types from Vietnam and Korea. You could get fresh ones but it is convenient to use the dried varieties since they have a longer shelf-life.

Egg noodles, *bee hoon* (rice vermicelli), *tung hoon* (glass noodles) and *mee sua* (wheat vermicelli), all come in dried form. *Bee hoon* and *tung hoon* should be well-soaked in cold water before cooking. Soak *bee hoon* for about 2 hours till the folded noodles, which tend to stick together, separate. *Bee hoon* for frying should not be boiled, otherwise they will break into short lengths when fried. *Tung hoon* will soften after soaking in room temperature for about half an hour. Soak in hot water if you are in a rush. *Mee suah* should be soaked in boiling water to soften it just before cooking.

Eggs noodles, which are yellow and made with wheat flour, are sold fresh but some also come in the dried form. Nowadays, fresh egg noodles are widely available even in most supermarkets in Britain. It is also known as Hokkien *mee*. Fine egg noodles are also known as *wonton* noodles.

Yee foo mee is a Cantonese deep-fried egg noodle that comes in a packet. They are crispy and should not be soaked in water before cooking.

Koay teow (flat rice noodles) can be bought fresh or in the dried form. Fresh *koay teow* cannot be kept for

From top middle, clockwise:
yee foo mee,
dried koay teow,
fresh koay teow,
glass noodles,
fresh hor fun,
wonton noodles,
bee hoon.

Middle:
mee sua

long so I find it convenient to buy the dry variety. Dried *koay teow* must be soaked in boiling water till it softens, but it should not be boiled. Drain the water only just before cooking.

Hor fun is a similar to *koay teow* but is wider and not as soft.

Bee hoon, *hor fun* and *koay teow* are predominantly made of rice. *Tung hoon* or glass noodles are predominantly made of green beans, hence they are gluten free.

Meat, cooked and uncooked, prawns, fish balls, fish cakes, Chinese sausage, canned meat, canned vegetarian food like *loh han chye* and eggs can be fried with noodles.

Vegetables that are commonly used in noodle dishes are beansprouts, carrots, cabbage, *peh chye* (Chinese cabbage), chives and green vegetables like *chai sim* (Chinese flowering cabbage) and broccoli.

Fried sliced shallots, *fu chok* or *tek ga kee* (fried sweet soya bean stick), sliced lettuce, spring onions, pickled sliced chillies and *sambal belacan* are some of the condiment that accompany noodles.

The portions of noodle dishes in this chapter are mostly for two persons. However, when canned food is used, the servings are adjusted to use up all the contents of the can.

Fried Hor Fun or Bee Hoon
2 Portions

This is a Cantonese dish. I grew up in my grandmother's house in Macalister Road in Penang and there was a stall diagonally opposite the house at the junction of Lorong Selamat that sold fried hor fun *and* Yee Foo Mee. *This recipe is based on my early observations of how it was prepared.*

It is best to use fresh hor fun. *Sheets of* hor fun *are normally stacked and then cut into strips. It is easier to separate the strips when it is fresh, before being kept in the fridge. If refrigerated, it is best to let it come to room temperature before cooking.*

If you are cooking more than two portions of this dish, it is best to fry no more than two portions of hor fun *at a time to get the* wok hei – *the desired and characteristic charred taste of fried dishes – unless you have a very hot stove.*

The sauce for the hor fun, *however, can be cooked all at once.*

Char siew *or* siew bak *can be used in place of fresh meat or fish.*

240 g *hor fun* or 100 g dry *bee hoon* (see note on page 64)
4 cloves garlic
4 tsps oil
80 g beansprouts, optional
2 tsps light soya sauce
2 eggs

Sauce
6 mushrooms, soaked in water if dried ones are used
100 g green vegetables
80 g carrots
8 prawns
100 g meat or fish
1 tsp light soya sauce
4 tsps cornflour
600 ml water with half a chicken stock cube or stock

If the *hor fun* has been refrigerated, allow it to come to room temperature. Separate the strips of *hor fun*.

Smash the garlic, skin and chop finely. Divide into two equal portions.

Slice the mushrooms. Rinse and cut up the vegetables. Separate the stalk from the leaves. Rinse the carrots and slice thinly.

Remove the head and shells of the prawns and devein. Cut the meat into thin slices. If fish is used, slice thickly. Marinate with the light soya sauce.

Render 4 teaspoons of cornflour in 4 tablespoons of water in a bowl and add a pinch of salt.

Heat up a wok. When it is hot, add 2 teaspoons of oil. Add one portion of the chopped garlic and fry till light golden brown. Put in the beansprouts, if using, and then the *hor fun* together with 2 teaspoons of light soya sauce. The heat of the stove should be on full blast.

Stir the ingredients thoroughly and leave for about 1 minute so that the *hor fun* is slightly charred. Then turn the *hor fun* over and leave for about a minute or so. Give the *hor fun* a good stir. Turn the heat down to medium.

Now push the *hor fun* to the side of the wok, forming a well. Break the eggs in the centre of the wok. Scramble the eggs and mix with the *hor fun*. When the eggs are cooked, move the mixture to a serving plate.

Heat up the wok again. When it is hot, add 2 teaspoons of oil. Add the remaining chopped garlic and the prawns, then stir. Include the sliced carrots and continue stirring. Keep stirring for about one minute, then add the mushrooms and continue to stir for one or two minutes until the carrot is nearly cooked and has lost its bright orange colour.

Add in the 600 ml of water with chicken cube or the stock, stir, and wait for the sauce to boil. Allow to simmer for about a minute.

Stir the cornflour and water mixture and add to the marinated meat or fish. Mix well, pour into the wok and give it a good stir. The sauce is ready when it becomes more translucent.

Pour the sauce over the *hor fun* on the serving plate and serve.

Note: Depending on its thickness, 100 g of *bee hoon* will become about 240 g after it is soaked in water.

Dry Fried Mee, Bee Hoon or Bee Hoon Mee
2 Portions

240 g Hokkien *mee*, blanched, or 100 g dry *bee hoon*
  or for *bee hoon mee*, 120 g Hokkien *mee*, blanched, and 50 g dry *bee hoon*
100 g vegetables, a mix of beansprouts, green vegetables and snow peas
160 g meat of any kind
8 -12 prawns
2 tsps oil
60 g onions, peeled and sliced
4 tsps light soya sauce
2 eggs
Fried shallots
Sambal belacan

If using *bee hoon*, soak it in 1.5 litres of warm water for at least 1 hour, preferably 2. Dry *bee hoon* will more than double in weight after soaking.

Wash and prepare the vegetables. If using snow peas, string them to remove the fibrous strips on the sides of the pods (see page 23). Set aside.

Cut the meat into thin slices. Remove the heads and shells of fresh prawns and devein. If using frozen prawns, thaw by soaking in water.

Heat a wok and, when it is hot, put in the oil. Add the sliced onions and fry till transparent. Include the prawns and give a good stir. Then put in the sliced meat and the soya sauce. Stir till the prawns are no longer transparent.

Add the Hokkien *mee* and/or the soaked *bee hoon*. Thoroughly mix the noodles with the other ingredients using chopsticks and a frying ladle. If using *bee hoon*, mix till its colour is even without any white patches.

Now add the beansprouts and the vegetables and continue to stir. When the vegetables are cooked, having turned a darker green, push the noodles to the side of the wok to form a well in the middle.

Add 1 teaspoon of oil, and when the oil sizzles, crack the eggs into the wok. Break up the eggs with a ladle and when the whites are cooked and have turned white, thoroughly mix the eggs with the noodles using chopsticks.

Serve with fried shallots, *sambal belacan* or chillies on the side.

Vegetarian Fried Mee or Bee Hoon

3 Portions

This is a convenient dish to cook if there is no meat available or you would like a vegetarian dish for a change. Various vegetarian canned food like mock duck, chicken and abalone made from gluten, lou han zhai *and* chai charng *(vegetarian intestines) can be used. They come in 250- to 300-g cans.. Mushrooms and green vegetables that are in season are added for a nutritionally balanced dish. You could choose to fry Hokkien* mee*, bee hoon or a combination of the two.*

360 g Hokkien *mee* or 200 g dry *bee hoon* or a mixture of 180 g Hokkien *mee* and 100 g dry *bee hoon* for *bee hoon mee*
75 g onions
150 g green vegetables or snap peas
250 g can vegetarian mock duck, chicken or abalone, or *lou han zhai*
10 fresh or dried mushrooms
Oil
2 tbsps light soya sauce
200 g beansprouts
2 eggs, optional
Fried shallots
Store-bought sliced pickled green chillies

If using *bee hoon*, soak it in enough warm water to cover the *bee hoon* for at least an hour, preferably two, till they are soft. If using Hokkien mee, pour boiling water onto the noodles in a container. Let it soak for one or two minutes, then drain the water and set aside.

Peel and slice the onions. Rinse and cut up the vegetables. If using snap peas, string the pods (see page 23). Set aside. Open the can of vegetarian mock meat or *lou han zhai*.

If using dried mushrooms, soak them in warm water for about 20 minutes, then drain. Rinse the mushrooms, slice them and leave aside.

Heat up a wok and, when it is hot, put in 1 teaspoon of oil. Then add the sliced onions and fry till they are transparent.

Empty the can of vegetarian ingredients into the wok and add the sliced mushroooms. When the liquid in the wok comes to a boil, add the light soya sauce and the noodles.

Thoroughly mix the noodles with the other ingredients in the wok using a pair of chopsticks and frying ladle. There should be some liquid at the bottom of the wok. If not, add 50 ml of water. If using *bee hoon*, continue to stir, making sure that it is mixed till its colour is even without any white patches.

Now add the beansprouts and the vegetables and continue to stir till the vegetables have turned a darker green and are cooked.

If eggs are used, push the noodles to the side of the wok to form a well in the middle. Add 1 teaspoon of oil and when the oil sizzles, crack the eggs into the wok. Break up the eggs with a frying ladle and when the egg whites have cooked till they turned white, thoroughly mix the eggs with the noodles using chopsticks.

Serve with fried shallots and sliced pickled green chillies.

Hainanese Mee

2 Portions

Hainanese Mee is most probably a Hainanese adaptation of Hokkien Char from Penang, otherwise known as Hokkien Mee in other parts of Malaysia and Singapore. In Penang, it is traditionally served with a slightly watery sambal belacan *in Hainanese restaurants like Loke Thye Kee, Garden Hotel and the old Hollywood. In the past, the meat used was pork but, in more recent times, it has been replaced with chicken in halal establishments, especially in social and sports clubs in Malaysia.*

240 g Hokkien *mee*
4 cloves garlic
100 g green vegetables
8 prawns
100 g chicken
2 tbsps light soya sauce
2 tsps dark soya sauce
2 tsps cornflour
600 ml stock or water with ½ a chicken or vegetable cube
2 tsps oil
Fried sliced shallots
Sambal belacan

Pour boiling water onto the noodles in a container. Let it soak for one or two minutes, then drain and set aside.

Smash the garlic and remove the skin. Chop the garlic finely.

Rinse and cut up the vegetables. Separate the stalk from the leaves.

If using frozen prawns, thaw in water. If fresh prawns are used, remove the heads. Shell and devein.

Cut the chicken into thin strips. Marinate with the light and dark soya sauces.

Render the cornflour in stock or water with ½ a chicken or vegetable cube.

Heat up a wok. When it is hot, add 2 teaspoons of oil and fry the chopped garlic till light golden brown. Add the prawns and stir.

Put in the marinated chicken and continue to stir for about 2 minute or till the chicken turns whitish and is cooked.

Pour the cornflour slurry into the wok and give the ingredients a good stir. Wait for the sauce to boil, then add the vegetable stalks and the Hokkien *mee*. Mix well and simmer for about one or two minutes before incorporating the vegetable leaves with the noodles.

There should be gravy in the wok, otherwise add 2 or 3 tablespoons of water. The fried Hainanese Mee is ready to be served when the vegetables have turned a darker colour.

Serve with fried sliced shallots and *sambal belacan*.

Bee Hoon Fried with Canned Stewed Meat

3 Portions

I thought that this is our family recipe but found out that bee hoon *fried with canned pork leg and mushrooms is a very common dish among the Hokkiens. This fried* bee hoon *is wet with a bit of gravy. I use canned stewed pork ribs as the bones are bigger and easier to remove but some of the ribs are so soft that they can be eaten.*

400 g can stewed meat
150 g dry *bee hoon*, soaked in 1.5 litres of warm water for at least 1 hour
100 g beansprouts
100 g green vegetables
1 tsp oil
75 g onions, peeled and sliced
Fried shallots

Remove the hard bones from the stewed meat.

Rinse the beansprouts. Set aside.

Rinse and cut the green vegetables. Set aside.

Heat up a wok and, when it is hot, put in the oil. Then add the sliced onions and fry till they are transparent.

Add the stewed meat together with 150 ml of water. When the liquid has come to a boil, add the soaked *bee hoon*. Thoroughly mix the *bee hoon* with the stewed meat and its sauce with chopsticks and a frying ladle, making sure that it is mixed till its colour is even without any white patches.

Now add the beansprouts and the green vegetables and continue to stir. There should be some gravy, so add a few tablespoons of water if the dish becomes too dry. Adding water also prevents the *bee hoon* from sticking to the pan.

The fried *bee hoon* is ready to be served when the gravy boils.

Garnish with the fried shallots.

Yee Foo Mee
2 Portions

Yee foo mee *is wheat noodles which have been deep fried. This type of noodles is available in supermarkets in Malaysia, Singapore and the rest of Southeast Asia. Since it is deep-fried, it has a shorter shelf life compared to other dried noodles.*

This is the Yee Foo Mee that we could order with hor fun *at the stall at the junction of Macalister Road and Lorong Selamat in my young days. The gravy is cooked in much the same way as the* hor fun *recipe on page 63.*

For this recipe, prawns, chicken, siew bak *and* char siew *can be used. If using chicken, choose from fillet, breast or boneless thighs. Use a green vegetable like* chai sim, kai lan, *spinach, broccoli or French beans.*

80 g *yee foo mee*
2 cloves garlic
6 mushrooms, soaked in water if dried ones are used
100 g green vegetables
8 prawns
100 g chicken, optional
2 tbsps light soya sauce
60 g *char siew* or *siew bak*
4 tsps cornflour
Pinch of salt
2 tsps oil
600 ml water with ½ a chicken stock cube or 600 ml stock
2 eggs

Smash the garlic and remove the skin. Chop the garlic finely and divide into two equal portions.

Slice the mushrooms. Rinse and cut up the vegetables. Separate the stalks from the leaves.

Thaw the frozen prawns in water. If fresh prawns are used, remove the heads and shells. Devein.

Cut the chicken, if using, into thin strips. Marinate with the light soya sauce. Slice the *char siew* and *siew bak* into bite-sized pieces.

Render the 4 teaspoons of cornflour in 4 tablespoons of water in a bowl and add a pinch of salt.

Heat up a wok. When it is hot, add 2 teaspoons of oil. Add the chopped garlic and fry till light golden brown, then put in the prawns and stir again. When the prawns are translucent, add the vegetables and mushrooms and continue to stir for about a minute.

Pour in the 600 ml of water with ½ a chicken stock cube or stock, stir and wait for the sauce to boil. Allow to simmer for about two minutes.

If using chicken, stir the cornflour and water mixture and add to the marinated chicken. Mix well and pour into the wok and give it a good stir. When the sauce becomes translucent, add the *char siew* or *siew bak* and give it a good stir.

Break the eggs into the sauce and stir. Turn off the heat.

The sauce is ready when the egg white changes colour and becomes less transparent, though not fully cooked. If you like your Yee Foo Mee crispy, place the noodles on a serving plate and pour the sauce over. Otherwise, put the *yee foo mee* into the wok and cover with the gravy to braise.

Penang Char Koay Teow
1 Portion

This is the Penang version of Char Koay Teow which is a hawker dish. It is a not difficult to cook.

The thin, flat rice noodles are stir-fried with beansprouts, prawns, sliced Chinese sausages, eggs, cockles and Chinese chives in a very hot pan to get that special charred taste – wok hei. Traditionally, duck eggs are used.

At home, Penang Char Koay Teow should be fried in single portions as most household stoves cannot be hot enough to obtain wok hei *if the noodles are fried in large portions.*

130 g fresh *koay teow* or 65 g dried *koay teow*
5 prawns
2 cloves garlic
25 g Chinese sausage
3 stalks Chinese chives, optional
1 tsp chilli powder
3 tsps oil
50 g beansprouts
3 tsps light soya sauce
2 tbsps water with a pinch of salt
1 egg
Pepper to taste
10 cockles, optional

Fresh *koay teow* comes in sheets which are stacked and cut into strips. Separate the strips before frying. If using dried *koay teow*, bring a pot of water sufficient to cover all the dried *koay teow* to a boil. Put the *koay teow* into the boiling water and turn off the heat before the water boils again. Leave aside. Just before frying, strain the *koay teow* using a colander and rinse in cold water.

If using frozen prawns, thaw in water. For fresh prawns, remove the head and shells, then devein.

Smash the garlic and remove the skin. Chop the garlic finely. Thinly slice the Chinese sausage. Cut the Chinese chives, if using, into 3-cm lengths.

Mix the chilli powder with 4 teaspoons of water to make a smooth paste.

Heat a wok. When it is hot, spread 2 teaspoons of cooking oil in the wok. Put in the chopped garlic and fry till light golden brown. Include the prawns and fry till they are cooked.

Add the chilli paste and stir quickly. Now toss in the beansprouts, *koay teow* and 2 teaspoons of the light soya sauce. Stir well for 2 minutes, then add 1 tablespoon of the salted water.

Make a well in the middle of the wok by moving its contents to the side. Put 1 teaspoon of oil in the centre of the wok and break in an egg. Season with 1 teaspoon of light soya sauce and ground pepper. Partially scramble the egg and, when it is half cooked, mix it with the *koay teow*.

Sprinkle in another tablespoon of salted water, then add the sliced Chinese sausage, chives and cockles, if using. Give a good final stir for about one minute before turning off the fire. Serve hot.

Fried Tung Hoon

2 Portions

This is tung hoon *or bean vermicelli fried Hokkien style with meat and seafood – prawns, sliced fish and/or cuttlefish – in gravy.*

50 g *tung hoon* (glass noodles)
3 cloves garlic
100 g green vegetables
8 prawns
100 g chicken
2 tsps light soya sauce
2 tsps dark soya sauce
2 tsps cornflour
600 ml water
½ chicken or vegetable cube
1 tbsp oil

Soak the *tung hoon* in warm water for 20 minutes to soften it. Drain. Smash the garlic and remove the skin. Chop the garlic finely. Rinse and cut up the vegetables. Separate the stalks from the leaves.

If using frozen prawns, thaw in water. For fresh prawns, remove the head and shells, and devein. Cut the chicken into thin strips. Marinate with the light and dark soya sauces.

Render 2 teaspoons of cornflour in 600 ml of water with ½ a stock cube.

Heat up a wok. When it is hot, add the oil. Fry the chopped garlic till light golden brown, then add in the prawns and stir.

Put in the marinated chicken and continue to stir for about 2 minutes or till the chicken turns whitish and is cooked. Remove from the wok and set aside.

Pour the cornflour slurry into the wok and give the ingredients a good stir. When the sauce boils, add the vegetable stalks and the soaked *tung hoon* and mix well. Stir till the *tung hoon* is evenly brown.

Add the vegetable leaves and mix. There should be gravy in the wok, if not, add 3 tablespoons of water. Serve when the vegetables are a darker colour.

Mee Sua Soup
2 Portions

This is a simple, easy-to-cook dish which can be served as a soup or a one-dish meal. The main ingredients are mee sua *(wheat vermicelli), dried prawns and eggs. Fresh or thawed frozen prawns or fish can be used in place of dried prawns.*

Fresh chicken or other meat stock should be used if available, otherwise use chicken, ikan bilis *(anchovy), or vegetable stock cubes mixed with water.*

120 g *mee sua* (wheat vermicelli)
4 tsps dried prawns or 8 fresh prawns or 100 g fish
2 tsps oil
600 ml chicken or pork stock or 600 ml water with ½ a stock cube
2 tsps light soya sauce
2 eggs
Pepper to taste
Fried chopped garlic
Fried sliced shallots
2 red chillies, sliced

Pour boiling water over the *mee sua* in a large bowl. Stir the *mee sua* till it softens, then drain. Set aside.

Soak the dried prawns in water or, if using fresh prawns, remove the heads, shell, and devein. If using frozen fish, partially thaw, then slice.

Heat up the oil in a wok and fry the drained dried prawn or fresh prawns for about a minute, then add the stock and bring to a boil. Add the *mee sua* and fish, if using, and light soya sauce and stir.

When the soup is boiling, crack in the eggs. Submerge it in the soup to cook. If you like your yolk harder, cook it for longer.

Season with pepper, and serve with the fried sliced shallots, fried chopped garlic and sliced red chillies.

5: MAIN DISHES

In this chapter, the main dishes are grouped under four sections: Meat, vegetable, soups and curries.

In general, the majority of recipes here are designed for four persons but most of the dishes can be scaled up or down for more or fewer people. However, for some complicated dishes, it would be better to cook the full portion and keep it in the freezer or refrigerator.

Several of these main dishes are normally shared communally in a meal. The number of dishes served depends on the on the number of people eating and on family traditions. A simple meal for two may consist of a meat or curry dish and a vegetable or soup dish. More dishes would be served for a larger group.

MEAT DISHES

I have selected a variety of easy-to-prepare meat dishes and some complicated ones.

Aw Bak Chien, a family heirloom recipe, has been simplified.

Tau Eu Bak is not a difficult dish to cook, but it is important to pay attention to the details. The frills like the fried *tau kwa* can be omitted. Leftover Tau Eu Bak can be cooked with rice in a rice cooker to make "claypot" rice

My fried satay does away with the grilling but *char siew* still needs to be grilled in an toaster oven or oven. It is convenient to buy *siew bak* (roast pork) instead of roasting your own. Buy a bit more and use the leftovers to fry with garlic, which will revive the crispiness of the roast pork, to make the simple Penang restaurant dish.

Fried Chinese sausage, or *lap cheong* in Cantonese, will cook faster in a little oil if first steamed on top of rice. It also tastes so much better than the ones which have not been pre-steamed.

Chicken Fried with Sesame Oil and Ginger is a delicious dish traditionally prepared for mothers who have just given birth. Sesame oil is a common ingredient that enhances the flavour of dishes like porridge and Chicken Rice.

Clockwise from top: roast duck, char siew, Chinese sausage.

Fried Lap Cheong with Dark Soya Sauce

4 Portions

Lap cheong *is a very convenient and versatile food because it has a relatively long shelf life even if it is not stored in a refrigerator.*

An easy way to prepare lap cheong *is to boil it in water for about 10 minutes or to steam it on top of rice in a rice cooker once the rice cooker has automatically switched off. It can then be sliced at a slant and eaten with rice and a good quality dark soya sauce.* Lap cheong *tastes even better if it is shallow fried.*

Lap cheong *is also an ingredient for many dishes such as Penang Char Koay Teow, omelette and claypot rice.* Lap cheong *made with chicken meat is readily available these days.*

4 *lap cheong* (Chinese sausage)
1 tsp oil
1 tsp good-quality dark soya sauce

Place the sausages on the rice in a rice cooker just after the rice cooker has switched off. The *lap cheong* is ready after the rice is left to rest for 10 minutes.

Alternatively, you can boil the sausages in water for about 10 minutes till the skin has turned from transparent to a dull, pinkish white. Discard the water and, when the sausages have cooled down a little, remove the skin only if it has separated from the filling.

Heat up a pan, add a teaspoon of oil and shallow fry the sausages, turning them over again and again. Fry till there are brown specks of slightly burnt meat on the sausages and they smell good! This will take only a few minutes.

Slice the *lap cheong* at a slant. Transfer onto a plate and drizzle with the dark soya sauce. You could just eat *lap cheong* with plain rice or accompany them with sliced cucumber.

Tau Eu Bak
SOYA SAUCE BELLY PORK
4 Portions

Stewed meat or Tau Eu Bak in Hokkien is a popular dish for many families in Penang. It is a relatively simple dish to cook but takes a longer time to cook than most dishes in this book.

Belly pork is traditionally cooked with dark soya sauce, garlic, peppercorns and sugar. Fried firm bean curd and hard-boiled eggs are usually added but are optional. Chicken can be used instead of belly pork.

Tau Eu Bak tastes better if served the day after it is cooked. It goes well with rice because of the generous amount of gravy. Leftover Tau Eu Bak can be cooked with rice in a rice cooker to make a sort of claypot rice. Add mushrooms and vegetables like carrots for a more balanced meal.

This recipe uses a moderate amount of sugar, but some families prefer this dish to be sweeter.

Cook a full portion of this recipe and, if it is too much for a meal, freeze or refrigerate part of it.

400 g belly pork
2 eggs, optional
200 g *tau kua* (firm bean curd), optional
1 tbsp oil
2 tsps sugar
16 whole peppercorns
6 cloves garlic, smashed with side of chopper, leave skin intact
6 tbsps black soya sauce
150 ml water
Salt to taste

If using eggs, place them in a saucepan and pour in enough water to cover them. Remove the eggs. Bring the water to a boil, then turn off the heat. Carefully ease the eggs into the hot water and leave for about 12 minutes to hard boil. Drain and refill the saucepan with cold water. Let the eggs cool down but not till they are cold, then crack and carefully remove the shells and membrane. Cold eggs are difficult to shell.

Fry the *tau kua* if using. Heat a wok, and when it is hot, spread 1 tablespoon of oil to cover an area larger than the firm bean curd. Put in the bean curd and fry till one side is golden. Turn the bean curd over and fry till the other side is also golden. Cut the beancurd into quarters, then cut each quarter into four strips.

Cut the belly pork into 2-cm slices with skin on each piece. Then cut each slice into 2-cm pieces. Traditionally, the skin, which is rich in collagen, is left on for Tau Eu Bak. However, you may wish to trim away some of the fat. It is important to dry the meat before cooking, otherwise the sauce will be cloudy. If using chcken, cut into bite-sized pieces.

Heat up a tablespoon of fresh oil in the wok or reuse the oil used for frying the beancurd, spreading it evenly around, especially on the sides. This will ensure that the meat will not stick to the pan.

Add the sugar and stir until it caramelises – that is, when it melts and turns brown. Add the meat and fry for a few minutes, stirring constantly to ensure that it does not stick to the pan. Fry till most of the meat have been seared and nearly golden.

Add the peppercorns and the garlic and continue to fry until the garlic skin turns brown.

Include the black soya sauce and the 150 ml of water. Simmer on low heat for at least 30 minutes. If the sauce is too thick for your liking, add a few tablespoons of hot water.

Put in the bean curd; it will soak up the sauce. Add the boiled eggs, if using, before serving.

"Claypot" Rice with Leftover Tau Eu Bak

4 Portions

It is very convenient to cook claypot rice in a rice cooker.

However, you will need to understand how a rice cooker works. Rice cookers have a thermostat that automatically switches off the heater when the critical temperature is reached. At this point, the rice is only partially cooked. It will take at least another 10 minutes of resting time for the rice to fully absorb the water to be properly cooked.

If there are ingredients other than rice in the rice cooker, it could switch off earlier. This is likely to happen when cooking claypot rice with leftover Tau Eu Bak. Thus, to cook claypot rice in a rice cooker using this recipe, it is best to allow more time for the rice at the top of the pot to cook. However, the rice cooker will not switch on again till the temperature at the bottom of the pot has gone below the critical temperature.

Add two or three tablespoons of water to the side of the pot and stir to the bottom, then switch on the cooker again when the pot has cooled to below the critical temperature. Repeat this till the claypot rice is cooked.

The good thing is that by doing so, you are likely to have the delicious and crispy burnt rice crust or pnui phee *at the bottom of the pot. It is like the socarrat in Spanish paella.*

Cook a full portion of this recipe and, if it is too much for a meal, freeze or refrigerate part of it.

300 g raw rice
Leftover Tau Eu Bak
150 g chicken, fillet, breast or boneless thigh
2 tsps dark soya sauce
1 tsp light soya sauce
2 tsps sesame oil, optional
100 g *lap cheong* (Chinese sausage)
100 g carrots
6 mushrooms, dried or fresh, soaked in water if dried ones are used
150 g green vegetables
15 g salt fish (*tanau kiam hu* or bottled salt fish in oil), optional
Oil

Cut the chicken into slices of about 1 cm thick and marinate them with the light and dark soya sauces and the sesame oil, if using, for at least 2 hours.

Slice the Chinese sausage diagonally to 2 to 3 mm thickness.

Top and tail the carrots and cut the carrots into 1-cm thick discs.

Remove and the stalks of the mushrooms and cut the caps into quarters.

Rinse the vegetables, separate the leaves and stalks.

If using salt fish, put 1 tsp of oil in the rice cooker, turn on the rice cooker, then place the salt fish on the oil. Move the salt fish around the oil for about 2 minutes, then turn it over. The cooker will automatically switch off when the rice pot is too hot. Remove the salt fish from the rice cooker and break it into smaller pieces.

Wash and drain the rice. Add 2 cups (480 ml) of water.

Warm the leftover Tau Eu Bak and drain the sauce into a bowl. Add sufficient water to the sauce to make ½ cup (120 ml) of diluted sauce. Add this to the washed rice together with the prepared carrots and mushrooms in the rice cooker. Give it a stir and switch on the rice cooker and let it cook till the rice cooker automatically switches off.

Give the rice a good stir, especially at the bottom of the cooker. Spread the marinated chicken, sliced Chinese sausage and salt fish, if using, on the rice. Switch on the rice cooker again. If it doesn't switch on, wait for the rice to cool down before switching it on.

When the rice cooker has switched off automatically again, add 2-3 tablespoons of water around the side of the rice pot, then spread the vegetable stalks and then the leaves over the rice. Switch on the rice cooker once more. If it doesn't switch on, wait for the rice to cool down before switching it on.

When the rice cooker switches off automatically, leave it on the keep-warm mode for 15 to 30 minutes for the rice to be properly cooked. If the rice is still not fully cooked after that time, add 2 or 3 tablespoon of water around the side of the rice pot and switch on the cooker and wait for the rice cooker to automatically switch off again.

Aw Bak Chien
SOYA SAUCE PORK FILLET
4 Portions

This is the heirloom recipe of Aw Bak or Aw Bak Chien from my father's family. It is also a popular dish in many other families in Penang. Most probably of Hokkien origin, aw or black in the dialect refers to the black, shiny slices of cooked meat.

    The ingredients are basic: Pork fillet, black and light soya sauces, sugar, pepper, honey and oil. The use of pork fillet simplifies the cooking process as belly or shoulder cuts will take a much longer time to cook. Deboned chicken or beef fillet can also be used instead.

My mother had fried onion rings in her Aw Bak recipe, but they are not included in the versions served by some of my paternal aunts.

Aw Bak is similar to Babi Manis from Singapore. The latter uses calamansi lime or tamarind to impart a slightly sour taste and no oil is used.

I recommend frying rice to absorb the gravy left in the wok. The Aw Bak and onion rings go well with fried rice.

    Cook a full portion of this recipe and, if it is too much for a meal, freeze or refrigerate part of it.

250 g pork fillet
1½ tbsps light soya sauce
3 tbsps dark soya sauce
½ tsp pepper
1 tbsp sugar
150 g onions
2 tbsps oil
1½ tbsps honey

Cut the fillet across the grain into slices of 3-4 mm thick. Combine the two soya sauces, pepper and sugar and use the mixture to marinate the sliced meat for at least 30 minutes.

Peel the onions and cut them into ½-cm rings.

Heat up a wok and, when hot, add the oil. Spread the sliced onions in the wok and after about 10 seconds turn the onions over and fry for about

another 10 seconds. Keep the onion slices intact; do not separate into rings yet. Remove the onion slices from the wok and set them aside.

Put the marinated sliced meat into the hot wok and stir fry for about 3 to 5 minutes till the meat becomes a lighter colour. You will need to fry for longer if other cuts of meat are used. Add 3 tablespoons of water to the pan and stir with the meat to make a sauce. Simmer for about 4 to 5 minutes until the sauce has darkened.

Finally, spread the honey over the meat and mix thoroughly so that it covers every slice. Stir until the meat is dark, shiny and sticky. Now add the sliced onions and stir well. Spoon the sauce onto a serving plate and put the meat over the sauce. The Aw Bak is ready to be served.

To fry rice with the remaining sauce, put a cup of cooked rice and 2 tablespoon of water into the wok and mix with the sauce. Break in an egg and fry with the rice.

Fried Satay
4 Portions

This is a simplified version of satay which is fried instead of being skewered and grilled. It is a good dish to go with rice or as a filling for sandwiches and bread rolls. Lean meat is used. Pork is traditionally used but beef, lamb or chicken can also be used.

You could clean up the wok by frying leftover rice with the remaining sauce. Add a teaspoon of oil and scramble an egg and ¼ teaspoon of soya sauce with the rice.

Cook a full portion of this recipe and, if it is too much for a meal, freeze or refrigerate part of it.

250 g meat of your choice
1 tbsp light soya sauce
1 tbsp sugar
60 ml coconut milk or milk
50 g onions
1 tbsp oil
½ cucumber, sliced, optional

Ground spices
2 tsps coriander powder (*ketumbar*)
¼ tsp cumin powder (*jintan puteh*)
¼ tsp fennel powder (*jintan manis*)
1 tsp turmeric powder (*kunyit*)

Slice the meat into bite-size pieces of about ½ cm thick and 2 cm wide. Set aside.

Mix the ground spices with the soya sauce and sugar. Then add half of the coconut milk or milk and mix well to make a marinade.

Add the sliced meat to the marinade and mix it thoroughly. Leave aside to marinate for at least an hour, preferably overnight, in the refrigerator.

Peel and rinse the onion. Cut into quarters then slice into 3-mm pieces.

Heat up a wok and, when it is hot, spread the oil in the wok. Add the marinated meat and stir continuously with a frying ladle. When dry, add the

other half of the coconut milk and stir until the meat is slightly charred. Then add the sliced onions, stir and cook till the onions are slightly transparent.

Dish out and serve with sliced cucumber if you wish.

To fry rice with the remaining sauce in the wok, put in a cup of cooked rice and 2 tablespoon of water and mix with the sauce. When well-mixed, break in an egg and scramble it with the rice.

Note: You could replace the ground spices with 2 teaspoons of meat curry powder.

Char Siew
GRILLED MEAT
4 Portions

You will need a toaster oven to grill the meat, and an oven to cook the ribs. It will take a much longer time to cook if pork ribs are used instead of belly pork or chicken breast.

400 g belly pork, pork ribs or chicken breast
1 tbsp soy sauce
2 tsps Chinese rice wine or sherry
½ tsp sesame oil
2 tsps honey
½ tsp five-spice powder
2 cloves garlic, crushed or grated
1 cm ginger, grated

Cut the belly pork or chicken breast into 2-cm slices. Remove the skin if any. If using ribs, cut into pieces between the ribs.

Mix the soy sauce, Chinese rice wine or sherry, sesame oil, honey, five-spice powder, garlic and ginger to make a marinade. Stir to mix well. Rub the marinade over the slices of meat and set aside for at least one hour or, preferably, overnight in the refrigerator.

Spread out the meat on an oven tray and place it in a toaster oven to grill for about 10 minutes. Make sure it is not burnt. Turn the pieces over and grill for another 10 minutes.

If using pork ribs, marinate the ribs with the same marinade.

Preheat an oven to 165°C. Remove the ribs from marinade and place them on a roasting pan and cover tightly with aluminium foil.

Cook the ribs in the oven for one hour, turning occasionally. Increase the oven temperature to 200°C. Remove the foil from the pan and bake the ribs for 10 minutes, turning once, until they are nicely browned.

Fried Siew Bak with Garlic

FRIED ROAST PORK WITH GARLIC

4 Portions

This is a simple dish of siew bak or roast pork jazzed up by frying it with garlic, dried chillies, soya sauce and sugar. It is one of the dishes served at the Tek Sen restaurant at Carnarvon Street in Penang. The restaurant was awarded a Michelin Bib Gourmand award for 2023.

Buy ready-made roast pork for this dish.

200 g roast pork
4 dried chillies, optional
2 cloves garlic
2 tsps oil
2 tsps light soy sauce
1 tsp sugar

Cut the roast pork into bite-sized slices of about 1.5 cm thick. Set aside.

If using dried chillies, remove the stalks and cut the chillies into 2 or 3 pieces. Shake out the seeds and soak the chillies in water till they have softened.

Smash the garlic, remove the skin and chop the garlic finely. Keep aside.

Heat up a wok, then add the oil. When it is smoking hot, put in the chopped roast meat and fry till crispy. Move the roast meat to the side of the wok. Add the dried chillies, if using, and stir fry. Stir in the chopped garlic when the chillies become pungent.

Bring the roast meat back to the centre of the pan and mix with the garlic and chillies. Fry till the garlic is golden, then put in the light soya sauce and sugar to thoroughly mix with the meat. Stir for about a minute. Turn off the heat and transfer the fried *siew bak* to a plate.

Mua Eu Kay

CHICKEN FRIED WITH SESAME OIL AND GINGER
4 Portions

This is a traditional dish for mothers during their post-natal confinement period, but it is delicious and enjoyed by everyone. The recipe is simple and easy to cook. Buy chicken fillet or breast if you are not confident about deboning chicken.

250 g chicken fillet or breast or wings or legs, de-boned
2 tsps soya sauce
2 tsps Chinese rice wine or sherry
20 g old ginger
2 cloves garlic
1 tsp oil
1 tsp sesame oil

Slice the chicken into bite-size pieces about ½-cm thick and 2 to 3 cm wide. Set aside.

Mix the soya sauce and Chinese rice wine or sherry and marinate the chicken with it. Set aside for at least half an hour.

Scrape off the skin of the ginger with the blunt edge of a knife. Slice the ginger thinly and set aside.

Lightly smash the garlic, remove the skin, and chop the garlic.

Heat up a wok, put in the oil and the chopped garlic. Saute till fragrant, then add the marinated chicken and the sliced ginger. Stir fry for about 3 minute. Add 2 tablespoons of water for some gravy. Finally, stir in the sesame oil.

Egg Belanda
SWEET, SOUR AND SAVOURY FRIED EGG
4 Portions

Egg Belanda is a simple, sweet, sour and savoury dish. There are other belanda dishes cooked with fried fish, salt fish, eggplant, prawns or belly pork instead of egg. Some recipes include belacan (shrimp paste).

Egg Tempra is most probably the southern Nonya equivalent of this nothern Nonya dish with a small difference – tamarind is used by the northern Nonyas while the southern Peranakans tend to use lime juice for the slightly sourish taste. The southern version is also darker, due to dark soya sauce used, setting it apart from the northern version.

In the past, dishes, fruits and vegetables associated with the Europeans were often described as "Dutch" or "Belanda" in Kristang, the Dutch and Portuguese creole. Tempra is the term for spices or condiments in Kristang. Whatever the origin, this dish is cooked at home by the Nonyas and Eurasian families of the Straits Settlements: Singapore, Malacca and Penang.

2 tsps *assam Jawa* (tamarind), or 4 tsps lemon or lime juice, or 2 tsps vinegar
4 cloves garlic
8 shallots
2 red chillies or small red peppers
4 tsps oil
4 eggs
2 tbsps light soya sauce
1 tsp dark soya sauce
2 tsps sugar
200 ml water

Use your fingers to render the tamarind in about 4 tablespoons of water. Pick out or sieve to remove the pulp and discard it. Set aside the tamarind water.

Cut off the root end of the garlic cloves and remove the skins. Cut the garlic into slices of about 1-2 mm thick.

Peel and rinse the shallots. Cut into thin slices from top to bottom.

Cut off the stalk of the chillies or red peppers. Cut the chillies or red peppers into two from the stalk downwards. Remove the seeds and the centres. Slice the chillies or peppers into pieces of about 1 x 2 cm.

Heat up a wok or small pan. Add the oil and fry the sliced garlic till light brown. Transfer the fried garlic onto a plate. Use the same oil to fry half of the sliced shallots. Stir the shallots constantly to ensure that they are cooked evenly. When light golden brown, turn down the heat and transfer the fried shallots to the plate with the garlic.

Heat up the pan again and fry the eggs with the remaining oil. When the yolks change to a lighter colour, turn the eggs over. The eggs are ready when the yolks just harden. Remove the eggs from the pan.

Fry the other half portion of the sliced shallots till the shallots are transparent. Then add the red chillies or peppers together with the soya sauces, the tamarind water and sugar. Once the ingredients are well mixed, add the water. When the gravy boils, add the eggs and bathe them in the gravy.

Garnish with the fried sliced shallot and garlic. Serve.

VEGETABLE DISHES

I have chosen some simple-to-prepare vegetable dishes like Fried Beansprouts which use few ingredients, Fried Firm Soya Bean Cake with Beansprouts which is an upgrade of the basic dish, and Fried Bean Curd with Vegetables which is more complex.

Fried Cabbage with Crab Meat introduces new cooks to crab meat – an 'exotic' ingredient though frozen or canned crab meat is commonly found today.

I have also included my mother's Min Chee recipe but have modified it to include readily available mixed vegetables so that it is closer to the version offered by Penang Hainanese restaurants. I have noted that most frozen mixed vegetables include sweetcorn which traditional Min Chee does not have.

Fried Beansprouts
4 Portions

Beansprouts can be simply fried with chopped up garlic. You can add spring onions or chives. Sliced red chilli will give it colour and oomph!

This dish will be greatly enhanced if fried sliced salt fish is added. The best salt fish to use is tanau kiam hu *made from Ikan Kurau (Threadfin). Salt fish bottled in oil, which have a long shelf life, is also suitable.*

400 g beansprouts
2 cloves garlic
4 stalks spring onions or chives
2 medium-sized red chillies, optional
20 g salt fish, optional
2 tsps oil
2 tsps light soya sauce

Rinse the beansprouts and remove the black husks, if any.

Smash the garlic and remove the skin. Chop the garlic finely and set aside.

Wash the spring onions or chives, discarding any wilted leaves. Cut the spring onions or chives into lengths of about 3 cm.

If using chillies, remove the stalks and slice the chillies diagonally into long strips.

Cut the salt fish, if using, into 3-4 cm slices.

Heat up a wok, then add the oil. If using salt fish, fry them until fragrant and golden brown, then remove and set aside.

Fry the garlic till golden brown then add the beansprouts and light soya sauce. Stir for about one minute till the beansprouts just become translucent, then add the spring onions or chives. Give the mixture a good stir and transfer to serving plate.

Break up the fried salt fish, if using, and sprinkle over the beansprouts.

If using sliced chillies, spread them over the dish.

Fried Firm Soya Bean Cake with Beansprouts

4 Portions

150 g beansprouts
250 g *tau kwa* (firm soya bean cake)
4 stalks spring onions
40 g shallots
2 tbsps *tau cheow* (preserved soya beans)
1 tsp sugar
100 g prawns
2 tbsps oil

Soak the beansprouts in water and remove the black husks, if any. Drain and set the beansprouts aside.

Wash the spring onions, discarding any wilted leaves. Cut the spring onions into 3-cm lengths.

Peel the shallots. Wash and cut them into slices of about 1-mm.

Divide the preserved soya beans into two portions. Finely mash up one portion and roughly mash up the other. Combine and add the sugar.

Wash the prawns. Remove the heads, peel and devein. Rinse the prawns.

Cut the firm soya bean cake into slices of about ½-cm thick.

Heat a wok and, when hot, add 1 tablespoon of the oil. Place the sliced firm soya bean cake on the wok without overlapping and fry. When golden brown, turn over to fry the other side till golden brown. Drain the oil and set the firm soya bean cake aside in a plate.

Put the remaining 1 tablespoon of oil in the wok. When hot, add the sliced shallot and fry till golden brown but not charred.

Move the shallots to the edge of the wok and put in the preserved soya bean mixture. Fry till fragrant, and add a tablespoon of water if too dry. Add the prawns. Mix with the preserved soya beans and stir in the fried shallots.

Add the fried firm soya bean cake and 150 ml of water. Stir to mix well. Include the beansprouts and the spring onions and bring to a boil. Serve.

Fried Bean Curd with Vegetables
4 Portions

This tofu dish is fried in the Cantonese style. Traditionally, tofu was sold in square slabs but, today, it also comes in cylindrical or rectangular plastic packs. For the cylindrical ones, you have a choice of the traditional plain white variety or the yellowish egg tofu.

For this recipe, you can use prawns, meat, chicken and char siew. *It is more convenient to use frozen prawns as there is no need to remove the heads and shells or to devein. For chicken, use fillet, breast or boneless thighs. Any lean meat can be used.*

For vegetables, use carrots, fresh or dried mushrooms, sweet peas, snow peas or a green vegetable like chai sim *(Chinese flowering cabbage) or* kai lan *(Chinese broccoli). Spinach, cauliflower and broccoli are other choices.*

200 g tofu
2 cloves garlic
100 g carrots
8 fresh button mushrooms or dried mushroom, soaked in water
80 g sweet peas or snow peas
100 g green vegetables
8 prawns
100 g chicken fillet
2 tbsps light soya sauce
4 tsps cornflour
Salt to taste
4 tsps oil
600 ml stock or water with ½ a chicken, vegetable or *ikan bilis* (anchovy) stock cube
2 eggs

For tofu in rectangular packaging, cut into 1-cm slices and then cut each slice into two. If using cylindrical tofu, cut the plastic roll into half. Cut off the plastic packaging at both ends and ease the tofu out of its plastic casing. Cut the tofu into cylindrical slices of about 1-cm thickness.

Smash the garlic, remove the skin and chop the garlic finely. Divide into two equal portions.

Slice the carrots thinly. Slice the mushrooms.

Top and tail the pea pods and string to remove the fibrous edges (see page 23).

Wash and cut up the vegetables. Separate the stalk from the leaves.

Thaw the frozen prawns in water. If using fresh prawns, remove the head and shells, and devein.

Cut the chicken fillet into 3-mm strips. Marinate with the light soya sauce.

Render 4 teaspoons of cornflour in 4 tablespoons of water in a bowl and add a pinch of salt.

Heat up a wok. When it is hot, add the oil and fry the chopped garlic till golden.

Add the prawns and fry till they are translucent, then add the mushrooms and carrots and continue to stir for one or two minutes till the colour of the mushroom darken.

Pour in the 600 ml of stock, stir, and wait for the sauce to boil. Add the vegetables and bring to a boil, then lower the heat and allow to simmer for about one to two minutes.

Meanwhile, stir the cornflour and water, and add the mixture to the marinated sliced chicken. Put all of this into the wok and give it a good stir. The sauce is ready when it becomes translucent. Add the pieces of tofu and carefully mix with the sauce without breaking them.

Finally, break in the eggs and stir thoroughly into the sauce. Turn off the heat. Continue to cook in the residual heat till the egg white turns white. Serve.

Min Chee

DICED MEAT AND VEGETABLES
4 Portions

Min Chee or Bin Chee is a unique home-cooked and Western-style Hainanese cum nonya restaurant dish from Penang. The home-cooked version is simpler, using minced meat (usually pork or chicken), diced potato and onions. The restaurant version adds canned button mushrooms, diced carrots and peas, and is served with fried egg, mashed potato, croutons, and fried sliced shallots with Worcestershire sauce as a condiment.

For this easy-to-cook version, I added mushrooms and frozen mixed vegetables to the home-cooked recipe. The use of frozen mixed vegetables cuts out the dicing of the carrots, but adds sweet corn, which is in most frozen mixed vegetables today. Sweet corn is not traditionally included in Min Chee.

For vegetarians, a plant-based protein could be used instead of minced meat.

200 g coarsely minced chicken or pork
3 tsps light soya sauce
Pepper to taste
50 g potatoes
250 ml water
100 g onions
100 g frozen mixed vegetables
60 g button mushrooms, canned or fresh
4 tsps oil
6 cm cinnamon stick
8 cloves
Salt to taste
Worcestershire sauce
Croutons

Mix the light soya sauce and pepper with the minced meat, making sure that the mince is not lumpy.

Peel and dice the potatoes into ½-cm cubes. Boil or microwave in 250 ml of water till just soft but not overcooked. Set aside.

Peel the onions and dice into ½-cm cubes.

Thaw the frozen mixed vegetables by soaking in water, then drain.

Dice the mushrooms into ½-cm cubes.

Heat up a wok and, when hot, put in the oil. Add about a quarter of the diced onions and fry for about a minute till slightly transparent. Include the cinnamon stick, cloves, salt and the marinated minced meat.

Stir well to break up the mince, ensuring that there are no large lumps. The meat is cooked when it turns whitish for chicken or whitish grey for pork.

Stir in the diced mushrooms and fry for about 1 minute. Then add the rest of the diced onions and stir.

Add the boiled diced potato and mix well with the minced meat and onions. Include the thawed mixed vegetables and give a good stir.

Simmer for a few minutes until the diced onions are soft. Transfer to a serving plate and serve with Worcestershire sauce, fried sliced shallots and croutons.

Fried Cabbage with Crab Meat
4 Portions

This is a simple, iconic Penang dish served in the old Hainanese restaurants of yesteryear like Spring Tide next to the old Chinese Swimming Club, Sin Hai Kheng in Tanjong Bungah, and Sin Kheang Aun on Chulia Lane.

The main ingredients of this Hainanese Nonya dish are cabbage, onions and crab meat. You could use frozen or canned crab meat or else chopped-up prawns. Dried prawns can be used as a substitute.

The stems of some cabbage are bitter if not well cooked. To remove the thick stem, cut each leaf on either side of the stem. Slice the stems thinly to help them cook well, or discard them. If you have a choice, choose green cabbage rather than a white one.

250 g cabbage
100 g onions
100 g crab meat or prawns or 15 g dried prawns
2 tsps oil
1 tbsp light soya sauce

Detach the leaves of the cabbage. Rinse and drain them. Cut each leaf to remove the thick stem. Slice the stems thinly, if using. Stack the cut leaves and slice thinly.

Peel the onions. Rinse and cut them into two from the shoot to the roots. Then slice each half thinly along the same axis.

Thaw the crab meat if frozen. If frozen prawns are used, chop up and thaw. If using fresh prawns, remove the heads and shell and devein. If using dried prawns, soak them in 3 tablespoons of water for about 15 minutes, then drain, reserving the water.

Pre-heat a wok and add the oil. Stir fry about a quarter of the sliced onions and the crab meat, chopped prawns or the soaked prawns. Fry till fragrant, then add the rest of the sliced onions. Put in the sliced cabbage, light soya sauce and, if using, the dried prawns, the water used to soak them in, otherwise add 3 tablespoons of water. Fry the cabbage and onions till they become translucent. Stir in 3 tablespoons of water and simmer for about 3 minute or until the cabbage is soft. Serve.

Fried Luffa with Egg
4 Portions

For this dish, choose a young luffa because older luffa have more mature seeds which are too hard to be eaten and must therefore be discarded. Younger luffas are relatively heavier and have ridges that are higher.

It is best to use a vegetable peeler to skin the luffa. Cut the luffa into two, lengthwise. Remove the ridges and then the skin in between them.

If luffa is not available, you can use small zucchinis or courgettes but they must be sliced thinly because they take longer to cook. There is no need to peel the skin for courgettes.

400 g luffa
1 tbsp dried prawns
20 g small shallots
2 tsp oil
1 tbsp light soya sauce
2 eggs

Soak the dried prawns in about 3 tablespoons of water and set aside.

Cut the luffa into two, lengthwise, and remove the mature seeds which are yellow and hard. Peel off the skin of the luffa. Cut each half into two to four lengths. Cut each into ½ cm slices.

Peel the shallots and thinly slice them into rings.

Preheat a wok. Put in the oil and then the sliced shallots. Fry the shallots till golden, stirring continuously. Turn down the heat to prevent the shallots from burning. Transfer them to a plate and set aside.

Heat up the wok again and use the remaining oil to fry the soaked dried prawns. Stir for at least a minute or until the dried prawns are a bit brown. Add the sliced luffa with the light soya sauce. Stir fry for several minutes until the luffa becomes translucent. Add about 200 ml of water.

When the liquid in the wok has boiled, break in the eggs and stir to combine the egg with the luffa. When the egg white is no longer transparent, turn off the heat. Serve with the fried sliced shallots.

SOUPS

The secret to a good soup is a good stock. You can make your own stock by simply simmering bones or vegetables in approximately twice the amount of water by weight (e.g. 200 g of bones or vegetables in 400 ml of water) for about three hours.

For chicken soup, you could use the wings, legs and the innards if these come with the whole chicken. For a vegetable stock, you could use onions, carrots and/or celery. Otherwise, use chicken, vegetable or *ikan billis* (anchovy) stock cubes. I normally use about half a cube of about 5 to 6 g in about 500 ml of water.

For Chicken, Potato and Cabbage Soup and the Winter Melon Soup, you don't need to make a stock since chicken and pork ribs are already in the ingredients. For Egg and Glass Vermicelli Soup (Egg Drop Soup) and Wonton Soup, you will need a good stock for a tasty soup.

Chicken, Potato and Cabbage Soup
4 Portions

This is a simple soup that my mother used to make. If you like your cabbage soft, use the light green ones, otherwise use white cabbage, which are harder. You could add some carrots and goji berries to the soup. Goji berries add colour and, among other health benefits, is a powerful antioxidant and improves eyesight. It should be put in when the soup is nearly ready.

Make a full portion of this recipe and, if it is too much for one meal, freeze or refrigerate part of it.

350 g potatoes
250 g cabbage
500 g chicken
1 litre water
¼ tsp salt or to taste
1 tbsp goji berries, optional

Peel the potatoes and cut them into 4-cm chunks.

Detach the leaves of the cabbage, stack them up and cut the stack into six portions.

Cut the chicken into bite-size pieces.

Heat up the water. When it is boiling, add the chicken pieces. When the chicken pieces have turned to a lighter colour, add the potatoes. Bring to a boil, then turn down the heat to simmer.

Add the cut cabbage and stir the contents of the pot to ensure that the cabbage leaves are submerged in the soup. Simmer till the potatoes and the cabbage are soft. Serve.

Egg and Glass Vermicelli Soup

4 Portions

This is Egg Drop Soup or Egg Flower Soup. The egg is stirred into the soup to get strands of cooked egg.

Tung hoon is dried vermicelli made from green beans. The noodles have to be soaked in warm water to rehydrate them before cooking.

Tong chai in Penang Hokkien – pickled Chinese cabbage from Tianjin, China – is a distinguishing ingredient in this soup.

50 g *tung hoon* (glass vermicelli)
4 cloves garlic
4 tsps *tong chai* (pickled cabbage)
2 stalks spring onions
2 stalks coriander leaves
4 tsps oil
2 tbsp dried prawns
1.2 litre chicken stock or 1 chicken, vegetable or *ikan bilis* (anchovy) stock
 cube dissolved in 1.2 litres water
4 tsps light soya sauce
4 eggs
Mint leaves, optional
Pepper

Soak the *tung hoon* in warm water and set aside. Smash the garlic, remove the skin and chop the garlic finely. Chop the *tong chai* coarsely and set aside. Cut the spring onions into bits. Pluck the coriander leaves into short lengths.

Heat up the oil in a wok or saucepan. When the oil is hot, fry the chopped garlic till golden brown. Transfer the fried garlic to a small plate.

Add the dried prawns to the remaining oil and fry till fragrant. Pour in the stock and the light soya sauce and bring to the boil.

Break the eggs into a bowl and beat them. When the soup is boiling, pour in the beaten eggs and stir slowly to get strands of egg in the soup. If you like your egg with the yolk and white separate, do not beat the eggs.

Serve topped with the fried garlic and spring onions, coriander and mint leaves, if using. Season with pepper to taste.

Winter Melon Soup
4 Portions

Winter melon and pork ribs or chicken are the main ingredients of this simple soup. I have added dried scallops and goji berries to give it more flavour and colour.

Mature melons have hard seed which have to be removed, so it is best to buy a smaller and less mature melon so that you don't have to remove any seeds. Spaghetti melon is a good alternative for winter melon.

Make a full portion of this recipe and, if it is too much for one meal, freeze or refrigerate part of it for later.

500 g pork ribs or chicken parts
1.5 kg winter melon
30 g dried scallops
3 tbsps goji berries, optional
Salt to taste
Light soya sauce

Place the pork ribs or chicken parts in a container and pour in boiling water to cover them. Give it a good stir and drain away the water.

Boil 1.2 litres of water in a pot and add the blanched pork ribs or chicken parts. When the water starts to boil again, reduce the heat and simmer for about half an hour.

Cut the winter melon into discs of about 3-cm thick. Remove the skin and the hard seeds especially if they are dark-coloured. Cut each disc into segments of about 3 cm along the circumference.

Add the dried scallops and the cut melon to the stock and turn up the heat. Turn down the heat when the soup starts to boil. Simmer for about 20 minutes till the pieces of melon have softened. Add the goji berries, if using, and let the soup simmer for another 2 minutes. Add salt to taste.

Serve with light soya sauce as a condiment.

Boiled Wonton and Fried Wonton
Makes 50

Wonton *can be boiled and served in a soup with green vegetables. The soup is traditionally served with dry Wonton Mee also known as Konlo Mee. Since this is a hawker food, the* wonton *has very little meat filling. Wontons at higher-end stalls have prawns and other ingredients like wood ear fungus which gives the filling a crunch. An alternative is* sui kow *which has a filling made up mainly of prawns and minced pork.*

Fried wonton *is often served in restaurants as part of the cold platter that is the first course of a Chinese banquet. Otherwise, it is served in a sweet-and-sour sauce or, in a more elaborate version, with cucumber, onions, pineapple, peppers and tomatoes added. Fried* wontons *are also served in Konlo Mee.*

Wonton *skins can be bought in most supermarkets in Singapore, Malaysia and Southeast Asia. In Europe and the US, Chinese or Vietnamese stores will sell* wonton *skins.*

Wonton *skins can be frozen and thawed as required.*

50 *wonton* skins
150 g minced pork or meat of your choice
100 g prawns*
10 g wood ear fungus
5 stalks spring onions
2 tsps light soya sauce
1 tsp sesame oil
1 tsp cornflour or tapioca flour
Pepper

*If prawns are not used, increase the minced meat by 100 g.

Wonton

If using prawns, shell, devein and chop them up coarsely.

Soak the wood ear fungus in water for at least 15 minutes until it has expanded and softened. Rinse and cut into very thin slices of about 1 cm in length.

Cut the spring onions into 5-mm bits.

Mix the prepared wood ear fungus with the minced meat, chopped prawns, spring onions, light soya sauce, sesame oil, cornflour and pepper to taste.

Place a *wonton* skin with a corner facing upward on the palm of your hand or on a worktop. Put about 1 teaspoon of filling in the middle of the *wonton* skin. Dip a finger in water and wet the edges of the skin, then fold the skin downward over the filling to make a triangle with its base away from you. Press the edges of the skin to which you have put water to seal the *wonton*. Wet the top of the right corner of the triangle. Bring the left corner over the right corner to make the shape like a Chinese gold ingot. Press to seal. Repeat for the rest of the *wonton* skins and filling.

Alternatively, put 1 teaspoon of filling in the centre of the *wonton* skin, fold the edges of skin upward, gathering the skin together. Squeeze above the filling to seal the skin.

If you are deep frying *wonton*, you don't want to have a lump of filling at the bottom of the *wonton* and just skin at the top when wrapped. This will cause the skin on top to burn before the skin at the bottom becomes crispy. The solution is to simply seal the filling between two sheets of skin or fold the skin over filling to form a triangle and seal the edges together.

Boiling *Wonton*

Bring a large pot with at least 1.5 litres of water to a boil. Put in batches of about 10 *wontons* at a time so that the temperature of the water does not drop significantly. Boil each batch for about one to two minutes, stirring to prevent the *wontons* from sticking to the bottom of the pot. The *wontons* are ready when the skins become translucent. Remove the *wontons* from the boiling water using a colander with a handle and rinse in cold water. Set the *wontons* aside.

Deep-frying *Wonton*

Heat up a cup of oil in a wok until it is hot. Put in batches of about 10 *wontons* and deep-fry until golden brown. Remove from the oil using tongs or a pair of chopsticks and drain on paper towels. Repeat with the remaining *wontons*.

Wonton Soup
4 Portions

Wonton Soup is traditionally served with Konlo Mee but it can be served with other dishes in a meal. The wontons *for the soup and Konlo Mee are traditionally boiled, but can be deep-fried instead for a change.*

- 1 litre chicken or vegetable stock or 1 chicken, vegetable or *ikan billis* (anchovy) stock cube with 1 litre of water
- 200 g *chai sim* (Chinese flowering cabbage), *kai lan* (Chinese broccoli) or other green vegetable
- 24 *wontons*
- 4 stalks spring onion

Wash and cut up the vegetables. Separate the stalks from the leaves. Cut the spring onion into 5-mm bits.

Heat up the stock in a pot and, when boiling, put in the vegetables and the *wontons*. Cook till the *wonton* skins are translucent. Serve the soup and *wontons* garnished with the chopped spring onions

Soupy Wonton Mee and Konlo Mee
1 Portion

Fine egg noodles, also known as wonton mee *are used for Konlo Mee or dry* wonton *noodles, and soupy Wonton Mee.*

The noodles are sold in skeins of about 100 g. However, the weight is not standardised even in noodles made by the same manufacturer.

The quality of the noodles and the way they are prepared make the difference between a good and mediocre bowl of Wonton Mee. The noodles made in the Hong Kong style are preferred because they are more al dente or khew *in Hokkien.*

I grew up watching the hawkers going through the steps of preparing Wonton Mee but didn't understand their method. Then I found out what will happen when a whole skein is dropped into the boiling water. Therefore it is important to read and follow the instructions below for blanching the noodles carefully, otherwise you will end up in a mess!

It is best to use a large pot that can hold about 1.5 litres of water. This is to ensure that the temperature of the boiling water is not significantly reduced when the wontons *or noodles are added.*

Boil the wontons *then use the same water to blanch the noodles.*

Blanch one or two skeins of noodles at a time. Each skein must be loosened so that the strands are separate when they are boiled. Otherwise you will end up with a gluey lump of noodles stuck together.

Do not overcook the noodles; they should be al dente. Eat as soon as possible otherwise they would lose the al dente texture and clump together.

6 *wontons*
1 skein *wonton* noodles (fine egg noodles)
50 g *char siew* (grilled pork) or *siew bak* (roast pork)
50 g *chai sim* (Chinese flowering cabbage), *kai lan* (Chinese broccoli), or other green vegetable
½ tsp black soya sauce
¼ tsp light soya sauce
¼ tsp sesame oil
1 stalk spring onions, finely chopped
Pickled sliced green chillies, store bought

Cut the *char siew* or *siew bak* into slices of about 5-mm thickness.

Wash and cut up the green vegetables. Separate the stalk from the leaves.

Heat 1.5 litre of water in a large pot. Blanch the prepared vegetables in the boiling water and rinse in cold, running water. Set the vegetables aside.

Bring the water back to a boil for cooking the *wontons*. If you are preparing multiples of this recipe, cook them in batches of no more than 10 at a time. Gently stir to keep them from sticking to one another. Wait for the water to boil again. The *wontons* are ready when the skins become translucent; this should take one to two minutes. Remove the *wontons* from the boiling water using a colander with a handle and rinse them in cold water. Set aside.

Reheat the hot water used for cooking the *wontons*. When the water returns to a boil, loosen a skein of noodles into it and blanch for about 30 seconds and not more than a minute. We do not want to overcook the noodles. Once the noodles become shiny, scoop them out using a colander with a handle and cool them under cold, running tap water. The noodles are then drained before being quickly plunged into boiling water again. Scoop out and cool under cold, running water once more.

Place the blanched noodles in a bowl and top up with the soup. Add the vegetables, *wontons*, and slices of *char siew* or *siew bak*. Season with the light soya sauce, black soya sauce and sesame oil. Garnish with a teaspoon of the chopped spring onions.

For Konlo Mee, mix ¼ teaspoon light soya sauce, ½ teaspoon of the black soya sauce and ¼ teaspoon of sesame oil together. Spread the blanched noodles on a plate. Pour on the sauce and thoroughly mix with the noodles. Put the vegetables and the sliced *char siew* on top of the noodles. At hawker stalls, the *wontons* and sometimes the vegetables are served in the soup on the side. Garnish the noodles and the soup with the chopped spring onions.

A condiment of pickled chillies in light soya sauce is normally served with Konlo Mee and Soupy Wonton Mee.

Fried Wonton with Sweet-and-Sour Sauce
4 Portions

Fried wonton goes well with sweet-and-sour sauce which is known as lam siu *in Penang Hokkien. Although this recipe specifies cucumber, onions, capsicum and pineapples, you don't need to use all these ingredients. You could replace the capsicum with red chillies, or use carrots instead of cucumber. You could do away with the vegetables!*

Make a full portion of this recipe and, if it is too much for a meal, freeze or refrigerate part of it for later.

24 fried *wontons*
75 g cucumber
50 g onions
50 g capsicum
1 slice fresh pineapple or canned pineapple rings
2 tsps oil
2 cloves garlic, finely chopped
1 tsp vinegar

Sweet-and-Sour Sauce
3 tbsp tomato ketchup
1 tsp light soya sauce
1 tsp sugar
2 tsp corn flour
100 ml water

Mix well the ingredients for the sweet-and-sour sauce and set aside.

Cut the cucumber lengthwise into quarters. Slice off and discard the core. Gather the cucumber sticks and slice them into 2.5-cm lengths. Set aside.

Cut the onions into bite-sized pieces. Set aside.

Remove the stem and seeds of the capsicum. Cut the capsicum flesh into 2-cm squares. Set aside.

Cut the pineapple into bite-sized pieces. Set aside.

Heat up a wok and add 2 teaspoons of oil. Fry the chopped garlic till golden.

Add the onion, pineapple, cucumber and the vinegar and continue to stir fry. When the onion is transparent, add the capsicum and stir.

Pour in the sweet-and-sour sauce and continue to stir. When the sauce has thickened, transfer to a bowl to serve. Keep the fried *wontons* and the sauce separate. Pour the sauce over the fried *wontons* just before serving.

CURRIES

When I was a student in London in the 1960s and 1970s, commercial curry powders were not easily available there. Neither were seeds spices like coriander, fennel and cumin, so I could not even grind my own curry powders. I cooked curry using curry powder sent occasionally by my parents all the way from Penang. At that time Alagappa was the best-known brand of curry powder. There are numerous brands available now.

There are two main types of curry powders and pastes – for meat or fish. Vegetable curries use fish curry powder or paste.

The recipes below for fish, meat and vegetable curries are cooked using commercially prepared curry powders which require the addition of oil, onions or shallots and coconut milk or milk as a substitute. The curry powder has to be mixed with water to form a paste (*rempah*) and slow fried (*tumis*) with oil. The other ingredients are then added, with the coconut milk last.

Today, all-in-one instant curry pastes for different curries and other spicy dishes like Otak are more common than curry powders. You no longer need to *tumis* the *rempah*; you just heat up the curry paste, add the meat and water and simmer before finally adding coconut milk.

The curry sauce should not be watery but have a slightly viscous consistency so that it coats the meat.

Meat Curry using Curry Powder
4 Portions

Make a full portion of this recipe and, if it is too much for one meal, freeze or refrigerate part of it for later.

250 g lamb leg steak or chicken parts
25 g meat curry powder
60 g shallots or onions
2 cloves garlic
1.5 cm ginger
150 g potatoes
3 tbsps oil
1 star anise, optional
2 cm cinnamon stick, optional
2 cloves, optional
1 cardamon, crushed, optional
300 ml water
2 sprigs curry leaves, optional
40 ml coconut milk or milk
½ tsp salt or to taste

Cut the lamb leg steak into 2.5 cm cubes. Cut the chicken breast, if using, into serving pieces. Set aside.

Mix the meat curry powder in 100 ml of water to form a thin paste. Set aside.

Peel the shallots or onions, chop them up and set aside.

Smash the garlic with the flat of a knife, remove the skin and chop the garlic.

Scrape off the skin of the ginger with the blunt edge of a small knife and cut the ginger into fine sticks.

Peel the potatoes and cut them into 2.5-cm cubes.

Heat up a wok. Add the oil and when it starts smoking, fry the chopped shallots and garlic for about 3 minutes or till the shallots are transparent.

Add the curry paste and, if using, the star anise, cinnamon stick, cloves and cardamon. Saute for about 5 minutes. Add 2 tablespoon of water whenever the paste becomes too dry. It should be a thick liquid. If it becomes a lump like a dough or if it sticks to the wok, it is too dry.

Add 300 ml of water to the curry paste. Mix well and heat till the curry boils. Then stir in the meat. Lower the heat when the meat is cooked. Now put in the diced potatoes and simmer for about 10 minutes or till the potatoes are cooked. The potatoes are done when they can be easily pierced by a fork. Add the curry leaves, if using.

Add the coconut milk or milk to the curry and bring to a boil on low heat. Add another 50 ml of water if the curry is too dry. Taste, and add salt as required. Turn off the heat just as the curry begins to boil. The curry sauce should not be watery but have a slightly viscous consistency so that it coats the meat

The curry is ready to be served. However, it will taste better if it is left to stand for a few hours or overnight. Reheat before serving.

Meat Curry using Instant Curry Paste
2 Portions

I normally cook this curry with chicken and potatoes. For convenience, use chicken drumsticks, thighs or breasts or a combination of them. Other meats like lamb or beef can be used.

This curry is spicier than the other curries in this book.

One of the better all-in-one instant curry pastes is the A1 Mountain Globe brand. It is so good that your guests will not know that the curry is cooked using commercial curry paste! Be careful as there are other brands named just A1. The packaging for the A1 Mountain Globe paste sold in Malaysia and Singapore are not the same.

1 kg chicken parts
230 g packet instant meat curry paste
500 ml water
500 g potatoes
100 g coconut milk or milk

Cut the chicken breast, if using, into serving pieces.

Put the instant curry paste into a wok. Add the 500 ml of water, heat the wok, and bring to a boil.

Add the chicken parts to the curry sauce and stir well. When the sauce boils again, lower the heat and simmer until all the chicken pieces are cooked.

While the chicken is cooking, peel the potatoes and cut them into 2.5-cm cubes.

Put the potato into the curry and give it a stir. When the curry boils again, lower the heat and simmer until the potatoes are cooked. The potatoes are done when they can be easily pierced by a fork.

Stir in the coconut milk or milk and turn off the heat just before the curry boils. Transfer to a saucepan or a large container to cool. The curry is ready to be served. However, it will taste better if it is left to stand for a few hours or overnight. Reheat before serving.

Fish Curry using Curry Powder
4 Portions

It is more convenient to use frozen filleted fishes. In Malaysia and Singapore, fish such as mackerel, grouper, barramundi and sea bass can be used. Temperate fishes, such as haddock and pollock, are also suitable. I suggest you try different fishes and decide on what you like. You could advance from frozen to fresh fish which the fishmongers will gut and clean for you.

Make a full portion of this recipe and, if it is too much for one meal, freeze or refrigerate part of it for later.

250 g fish, mackerel, grouper, sea bass or haddock fillet
25 g fish curry powder
50 g onion
3 cloves garlic
75 g tomato
75 g ladies' fingers (okra)
3 tbsps oil
1 tbsp mixed *halba* (fenugreek) seeds, optional
1 tsp tamarind paste with seeds removed
3 green chillies, optional
3 sprigs curry leaves
40 ml coconut milk or milk
½ tsp salt or to taste

Slice the fish fillet into two or three pieces.

Mix the fish curry powder in 100 ml of water to form a paste and set aside.

Peel the onion, rinse and cut into two from shoot to root. Cut half an onion crosswise into thin slices of 3-mm thickness and set aside. Chop up the other half of the onion to fry with the curry paste. Set aside.

Remove the skin of the garlic and cut into 1-mm slices. Set aside.

Cut the tomato into quarters. Set aside.

Wash the lady's fingers and cut off the stems. Set the lady's fingers aside.

Heat up a wok. Add the oil and when it starts smoking, fry the sliced garlic till golden. Transfer them to a plate before they turn brown. Fry the chopped shallots in the same oil for about 3 minutes till they are transparent.

Add the curry paste and mixed *halba* seeds, if using. Saute for about 5 minutes. Add a tablespoon of water whenever the curry paste becomes dry. It should be a thick liquid. If it becomes a lump like dough or sticks to the wok, it is too dry.

Add 300 ml of water, the tamarind paste, the tomato, the sliced onions, green chillies, if using, and curry leaves. Heat till the curry boils, then lower the heat to simmer for another 5 minutes.

Add the ladies fingers, stir, and bring to a boil. Add the fish and bring to a boil again. Now lower the heat to simmer for a further 3 minutes till the fish is cooked.

Add the coconut milk or milk to the curry and bring to a boil on low heat. Add another 50 ml of water if the curry is too dry. Taste, and add salt as required. The curry sauce should not be watery but have a slightly viscous consistency so that it coats the meat. Turn off the heat just as the curry begins to boil.

The curry is ready to be served. However, it will taste better if it is left to stand for a few hours or overnight. Reheat before serving.

Vegetable Curry using Curry Powder

4 Portions

For this recipe, the fresh vegetables may be substituted with the more convenient and economical frozen vegetables or frozen mixed vegetables.
    Make a full portion of this recipe and, if it is too much for a meal, freeze or refrigerate part of it for later.

50 g lentils
25 g fish curry powder
100 g onions
2 cloves garlic
100 g potatoes
1 tomato
60 g carrots
60 g green beans or runner beans
60 g cauliflower
60 g peas
3 tbsp oil
50 ml coconut milk or milk
½ tsp salt or to taste

Soak the lentils for at least one hour, preferably overnight.

Mix the fish curry powder in 100 ml of water to form a paste. Set aside.

Peel the onions and cut them into two from the shoot to root. Cut each half crosswise into 2-mm slices and set aside.

Lightly smash the garlic, peel, and slice the garlic.

Peel the potatoes and cut them into 2.5-cm cubes.

Cut the tomato into into eighths.

Cut the carrots into quarters, lengthwise, and cut each piece into 2-cm lengths.

Top and tail the beans and cut into lengths of about 2 cm.

Cut the cauliflower into florets

Thaw the peas if using frozen peas.

Heat up a wok. Add the oil and when it starts smoking, fry the sliced onion and garlic till the onion is transparent. Add the curry paste and saute for about 5 minutes. Add 2 tablespoons of water if the spice paste becomes a lump or sticks to the wok. It should be a thick liquid.

Add the lentils, diced potato, tomato, and the other vegetables. Mix well with 300 ml of water and simmer for about 15 minutes or till the potatoes are cooked and can be easily pierced by a fork.

Add the coconut milk or milk and bring to a boil on low heat. Add 50ml of water if the curry is too dry. Taste, and add salt as required. Turn off the heat just as the curry begins to boil.

The curry is ready to be served. However, it will taste better if it is left to stand for a few hours or overnight. Reheat before serving.

6: DESSERTS

I have chosen five easy-to-prepare traditional home-cooked desserts that coincidentally have different origins. Southeast Asian ingredients are used, such as *gula melaka* or palm sugar and *santan* (coconut milk in Malay) which is used in place of diary cream.

Sago Gula Melaka, which most probably has origins in the Malay Archipelago, was popular among the British in colonial Malaya. The recipe appears in one of the earliest cookbooks of British Malaya, *The "Mems" Own Cookery Book* by Mrs W. E. Kinsey published in 1920. *Mem* is a term used to refer to European expatriate ladies of the house in colonial days. The objective of the cookbook was to help those *mems* manage their kitchen. I wonder if Mrs Kinsey modified semolina/rice pudding for her Gula Melaka Pudding or picked up the recipe from her kitchen helpers.

Green Bean Soup, or Lek Tau Thng in Hokkien, is a traditional Chinese dessert. It is a classic Chinese *tong sui* (sweet soup), together with Red Bean Soup (Ang Tau Thng). The difference between the two is that Green Bean Soup is cooling (yin) whilst Red Bean Soup is heaty (yang). The Malay version, known as Bubur Kacang Hijau (green bean porridge) includes coconut milk, rice or sago and even fruits, especially durian.

Gula melaka is used instead of demerara sugar. Demarara sugar, which is light brown, is partially refined but is free from harmful chemicals and preservatives and retains all the natural vitamins and minerals inherently present in cane sugar.

Sweet Potato Soup is another easy-to-cook dessert. It is traditionally cooked with ginger and demerara sugar. Sweet potatoes are nutritious and come in different colours.

Agar agar, *santan*, *gula melaka* – these three main ingredients form the name of a dessert which is commonly served in Malaysia and Indonesia. Agar agar is a gelling agent made from seaweed. It is used in Asia for desserts in place of gelatin which is made from animal bones.

Gula melaka gives a special flavour to this jelly. During the cooling process, the agar agar and the coconut will separate into two layers with the coconut milk on top. I have added sago to make it more interesting but it will take longer to prepare as the sago pearls take longer to cook. If you are trying out this recipe for the first time, you could leave out the sago so that the recipe is simpler and faster to prepare. This dessert is best served cold.

Kuih Ee is a Chinese festive dish served to mark the Winter solstice in the northern hemisphere around 21 and 22 December. We were told that we shall be one year older after eating Kuih Ee. In Hokkien, *ee* is round, referring to the shape of the glutinous rice balls in this dish. This dish is also served on Chap Goh Meh, the fifteenth and last day of Chinese New Year celebrations.

Sweet potato is readily available in most countries today. In addition, you only need ginger and demerara sugar to make Sweet Potato Soup.

Kuih Ee
GLUTINOUS RICE BALLS
4 Portions

Kuih Ee is made from a dough of ground glutinous rice. Small portions of the dough are rolled into balls which are boiled in water and then served in a ginger-flavoured syrup. Traditionally, bigger Kuih Ee, sometimes referred to ibu or mother, are white while the smaller ones are red. You may, of course, make red or white Kuih Ee in the same size.

For red Kuih Ee, use cochineal red food colouring to colour the dough.

For enthusiasts, you can make a half portion of Kuih Ee red and the remaining white.

Dough
100 g glutinous rice flour
¼ tsp sugar
100 ml water
10 drops red food colouring, optional

Syrup
500 ml water
75 g sugar
4 pandanus leaves, optional
20 g ginger, optional

Dough
Dissolve the sugar in the water.

Sieve the glutinous rice flour into a mixing bowl and gradually add the sugar water, stirring continuously. The dough is ready when it comes off the surface of the bowl. You may not need all the water specified in the recipe, depending on the quality of the glutinous rice flour, so do not use up all the water if the dough is wet. If too much water is used, the dough will have a shiny, wet look, in which case you need to add more glutinous rice flour.

If making red Kuih Ee, add the 10 drops of red colouring to the dough and knead thoroughly so that the colour is uniform. If making both red and white Kuih Ee, divide the dough into two equal portions. Put 5 drops of red colouring into one portion of dough and knead till the colour is uniform.

Keep the dough covered or transfer it into a plastic bag. Set aside for 3 hours or overnight in the fridge to allow the dough to relax. The dough can therefore be prepared earlier and stored in the refrigerator.

Syrup

Rinse the pandanus leaves and tie each into a knot, if used.

Clean the ginger, if using, and slice coarsely.

Boil the water, add the sugar and the ginger and the pandanus leaves, if using. If ginger is not used, the syrup is ready when it comes to a boil. Otherwise, simmer till the syrup is flavoured by the ginger.

Rolling the Kuih Ee

Allow the dough to return to room temperature if it has been kept in the refrigerator.

Knead the dough. Roll portions of the dough on a lightly floured surface with your palms into a rope of about 2 cm in diameter. Cut the rope into 2-cm portions. Repeat for the remaining dough. Roll each small portion of dough between the palms of your hands to form a ball.

If you wish to be traditional and make white and red Kuih Ee of different sizes, make the red dough into a rope of 1.5 cm in diameter. Cut it into 1.5-cm portions and roll into balls

Place the balls on a tray and cover with a cloth so that they don't dry out.

Boil at least 1 litre of water in a pot. Prepare at least another litre of cold water in a large bowl.

Transfer the white Kuih Ee into the boiling water. Scoop them out with a colander when they float and drop them in the cold water. Repeat for the red Kuih Ee if you have them.

Serve the Kuih Ee in the syrup, either hot or cold, in individual bowls.

Sago Gula Melaka
4 Portions

Sago Gula Melaka is a simple pudding made from sago and served with gula melaka syrup and coconut milk. Wendy Hutton, in her book, Singapore Food, described it as a favourite dessert of the colonial British after curry tiffin. The nearest English equivalent is rice pudding.

Rinsed sago is white. As the sago is cooked, the outside of the pearl becomes translucent and the white dot inside gets smaller. The sago will continue to cook after it has been removed from heat. So, do not overboil.

It is easier to dissolve the gula melaka if it is sliced thinly or chopped up before adding to the water. The liquid gula melaka will thicken when it has cooled down, more so if kept in the refrigerator.

50 g sago
75 g *gula melaka* with just over 1 tbsp of water
250 ml water
1½ tsps sugar
100 ml coconut milk

Fill a bowl with enough water to cover the sago. Stir well and drain by pouring the sago into a sieve.

Boil 250 ml of water and pour in the sago. Stir well and reduce the heat to let the sago simmer. Stir a few times to ensure that the sago does not stick to the bottom or side of the pot. If the mixture boils, turn off the heat for about a minute and then turn on the heat again to simmer. After about ten minutes, when most of the white dots in the sago pearls have reduced in size or disappeared, stir in the sugar. The mixture should be a thick liquid of sago pearls stuck together. It will thicken further when cooled in a refrigerator. Pour into a large bowl, or moulds, and cool before putting them in a fridge overnight.

To make the syrup, chop or slice the the *gula melaka* thinly. Heat up the *gula melaka* with just over 1 tablespoon of water in a pan over low heat. Stir till the *gula melaka* has dissolved into a clear, brown syrup, then remove from the heat. The *gula melaka* syrup will thicken slightly when it cools.

Serve the sago with coconut cream with a pinch of salt and *gula melaka*.

Green Bean Soup

4 Portions

Green Bean Soup is nutritious, and is a source of minerals, vitamins, protein and fibre.

120 g green beans
750 ml water
4 pandanus leaves, optional
3 tbsps demerara sugar

Rinse the beans and then soak them in water for about 2 hours.

Drain the green beans and put them in a saucepan with 750 ml of water. If using pandan leaves, tie each into a knot and put them in the saucepan. Bring to a boil, then reduce the heat to simmer for at least 30 minutes till the beans are soft and some of the beans have split.

Dissolve the demerara sugar in the soup and turn off the heat.

Green Bean Soup is best served warm.

Sweet Potato Soup
4 Portions

Huan Choo Thng is Hokkien for Sweet Potato Soup. It is a simple, traditional dessert of diced sweet potato boiled with old ginger and demerara sugar. The ginger gives the sweet potato a distinctive fragrance and a slightly spicy taste. Ginger is believed to help digestion and alleviate nausea.

Sweet potatoes come in various sizes and different colours. The flesh may be cream, yellow, orange or maroon. Consider using only one type of sweet potato for the soup because different sweet potatoes have different cooking times. The colour of the soup will not be clear, especially if the purple variety or a mixture of types is used.

This dessert is normally served hot or warm.

250 g sweet potatoes
35 g ginger
30 g demerara sugar
600 ml water

Skin the sweet potatoes and cut the flesh into cubes of about 2.5 cm. Soak them in water to prevent discolouration.

Rinse the ginger and cut it into slices of about 3-mm thickness.

Bring the water with the sliced ginger to a boil. Lower the heat and simmer for about 10 minutes.

Add the sweet potatoes and bring to the boil again. Lower the heat and simmer for another 10 minutes

Add the sugar and simmer for about 5 minutes or until the sweet potatoes are done, that is when they can be easily pierced by a fork.

Agar Agar Santan Gula Melaka

4 Portions

This is a simple dessert of agar agar, gula melaka *and coconut milk. The agar agar gives this dessert its bite while the* gula melaka *gives it the flavour. This recipe is based on my mother's, but I have added sago pearls to make it more interesting. However, If you are trying out this recipe for the first time, you could leave out the sago so that the recipe is simpler.*

It is best to use powdered agar agar as they dissolve faster than the strips of agar agar that were commonly used in the past.

5 g agar agar powder
350 ml cold water
5 g sago, optional
1 tsp sugar
A pinch of salt
75 g *gula melaka*
60 ml coconut milk
4 drops pandanus essence, optional

Dissolve the agar agar powder in 350 ml of cold water.

Soak the sago pearls, if using, in water and drain them. Set aside.

Bring the agar agar solution to a boil. Add the sugar, salt, *gula melaka* and sago, if using. Stir till the *gula melaka* has dissolved.

Pour in the coconut milk and stir thoroughly. Turn off the heat before it boils and mix in the pandanus essence, if using. Allow the mixture to simmer for 10 minutes or until the sago is transparent.

Pour the mixture into a jelly mould or soup bowls while it is hot. You may also choose to pour it into a 5-cm cake tin. Allow to set in a cool place, preferably in the refrigerator.

To serve, unmould the Agar Agar Santan Gula Melaka. Offer individual serving bowls or cut the agar agar in the tin into bite-sized squares or diamond shapes.

Index

Agar Agar Santan Gula Melaka 169
Aw Aw Nui 32
Aw Bak Chien 98

Beansprouts
  Fried Beansprouts 113, 115,
  Fried Firm Soya Bean Cake with
    Beansprouts 113, 117
Bee hoon 12, 61, 62, 63, 66, 68, 74
  Bee Hoon Fried with Canned Stewed
    Meat 74
  Dry Fried Mee, Bee Hoon or Bee Hoon
    Mee 66
  Fried Ho Fun or Bee Hoon 63
  Vegetarian Fried Mee or Bee Hoon 68
Bean curd (see Tofu)

Cantonese *chook* 48-49, 52
  Cooking Cantonese Chook in a Rice
    Cooker 52
  Cooking Chook without a Rice
    Cooker 52
Cantonese Restaurant-Style Fried Rice 45
Canned food 21, 38, 49, 62, 68, 74, 113, 121, 124, 143
Char Siew 35, 104
Chicken 10, 43, 91
  Chicken Fried with Sesame Oil and
    Ginger 89, 108
  Chicken Porridge 58
  Chicken, Potato and Cabbage Soup
    129, 130
  Chicken Fried with Sesame Oil and
    Ginger 89, 108
  Chicken Porridge 58
  "Claypot" Rice with Leftover
    Tau Eu Bak 95
  Meat Curry using Curry Powder 147
  Meat Curry using Instant Curry Paste 149
  Min Chee 121
  Mua Eu Kay 108
  Winter Melon Soup 135
Chinese cruellers 54, 56, 58

"Claypot" Rice with Leftover
  Tau Eu Bak 95
Crab 113
  Fried Cabbage with Crab Meat 113, 124
  Fu Yong Hai 38
Curries 24-25, 87, 145-155
  Fish Curry using Curry Powder 151
  Meat Curry using Curry Powder 147
  Meat Curry using Instant Curry
    Paste 149
  Vegetable Curry using Curry
    Powder 153
Curry paste 24-25, 145, 149
Curry powder 25, 145
Cutting and slicing techniques 13-23
  Broccoli, cutting 22-23
  Cabbage, cutting 20
  Carrots, cutting 15-16
  Cauliflower, cutting 23
  Chai sim, cutting 23
  Cutting with a knife or chopper 13-15
  Garlic, cutting 19
  Meat, cutting 23
  Mushroomss, cutting 21
  Onions, cutting 17-18
  Potatoes, cutting 16-17
  Shallots, cutting 20

Desserts 157-169
  Agar Agar Santan Gula Melaka 158, 169
  Glutinous Rice Balls 158, 159
  Green Bean Soup 157, 165
  Kuih Ee 158, 159
  Sago Gula Melaka 157, 163
  Sweet Potato Soup 158, 167
Diced Meat and Vegetables 121
Dry Fried Mee 66
Dry Fried Bee Hoon 66
Dry Fried Bee Hoon Mee 66

Egg noodles 12, 61, 66, 68, 71, 141
Eggs 27-40, 43, 49
  Aw Aw Nui 32
  Egg and Faux Shark Fin 27, 38

Egg and Glass Vermicelli Soup 129, 132
Egg Belanda 111
Egg Drop Soup 129, 132
Egg Sandwich 22, 27, 31
Fried Luffa with Egg 126
Fu Yong Hai 27, 36, 38
Hard-boiled eggs 27, 28, 31
Heirloom Scrambled Eggs 32, 49
Lap cheong Omelette 36
Omelettes 35, 36, 38, 49
Soft-boiled eggs 27, 28
Sweet, Sour and Savoury Fried Egg 111
Eu Char Koay 54, 56, 58

Fish 10, 84, 145, 151
   Fish Curry using Curry Powder 151
   Fish Porridge 56
Fish Porridge 56
Flat rice noodles 61, 79
Food handling 9-10
Food storage 9-10, 42
Fried Beancurd with Vegetables 113, 118
Fried Beansprouts 113, 115
Fried Bee Hoon 63, 74
Fried Cabbage with Crab Meat 113, 124
Fried Firm Soya Bean Cake with Beansprouts 113, 117
Fried Ho Fun 63
Fried Lap Cheong with Dark Soya Sauce 91
Fried Luffa with Egg 126
Fried rice 41, 43, 98
   Cantonese Restaurant-Style Fried Rice 45
   Nonya Sambal Fried Rice 46
Fried Roast Pork with Garlic 106
Fried Satay 89, 101
Fried Siew Bak with Garlic 106
Fried Tung Hoon 38, 82
Fried Wonton with Sweet and Sour Sauce 143
Frozen food 10
Frozen vegetables 121, 153
Frying
   Frying garlic or shallots 24
   Shallow frying 24
   Stir frying 24
Fu Yong Hai 27, 36, 38

Green Bean Soup 157, 165
Glass noodles 27, 38, 61, 62, 82, 132

Glutinous Rice Balls 158, 159
Hainanese Mee 71
Halal versions of dishes 71, 91, 93, 98, 101
Hawker food 71, 76, 79, 137, 141
Heirloom Scrambled Eggs 32
Ho fun 61, 62, 63
Hokkien *mee* 61, 66, 68, 71

Ingredients 12-13

Koay teow 12, 61-62, 79
Kuih Ee 158, 159

Lap cheong 35, 88-89, 91
   Fried Lap Cheong with Dark Soya Sauce 91
   Lap Cheong Omelette 36
Left over food 10, 41, 42, 89, 93, 95, 101
Luffa 126

Main dishes 87-155
Meat dishes 89-112
   Aw Bak Chien 89, 98
   Chicken Fried with Sesame Oil and Ginger 89, 108
   "Claypot" Rice with Leftover Tau Eu Bak 95
   Diced Meat and Vegetables (see Min Chee)
   Fried Lap Cheong with Dark Soya Sauce 91
   Fried Roast Pork with Garlic 106
   Fried Satay 89, 101
   Fried Siew Bak with Garlic 106
   Meat Curry using Curry Powder 147
   Meat Curry using Instant Curry Paste 149
   Min Chee 21, 113, 121
   Minced Meat Rice Porridge 54
   Mua Eu Kay 108
   Roast Pork 89, 104, 106
   Siew Bak 89, 104, 106
   Soya Sauce Belly Pork 89, 93, 95
   Soya Sauce Pork Fillet 98
   Tau Eu Bak 89, 93, 95
Mee sua 12, 61, 84
Mee Sua Soup 84
Min Chee 113, 121
Minced Meat Rice Porridge 54
Mise en place 25
Mua Eu Kay 108

Nonya food 46, 98, 111, 121, 124
Nonya Sambal Fried Rice 46
Noodles 61-85, 141
  Bee Hoon Fried with Canned Stewed Meat 74
  Dry Fried Mee, Bee Hoon or Bee Hoon Mee 66
  Dry Wonton Noodles 141
  Egg and Glass Vermicelli Soup 129, 132
  Fried Ho Fun or Bee Hoon 63
  Fried Tung Hoon 38, 82
  Fu Yong Hai 38
  Hainanese Mee 71
  Konlo Mee 137, 139, 141
  Mee Sua Soup 84
  Penang Char Koay Teow 79, 91
  Soupy Wonton Mee 141
  Vegetarian Fried Mee or Bee Hoon 68
  Yee Foo Mee 61, 63, 76
Noodles, types of 61-62, 63

Omelettes 27, 35, 36, 38, 49, 91
Ong family 7, 27, 32, 46, 98, 113, 130

Penang Char Koay Teow 79, 91

Rice 10, 41-43, 48, 50, 52, 89, 91, 93, 95, 98, 101
  Cantonese Restaurant-Style Fried Rice 45
  "Claypot" Rice with Leftover Tau Eu Bak 95
  Nonya Sambal Fried Rice 46
Rice cooker 11, 41-42, 50, 52, 89, 91, 93, 95
Rice, how to cook 41-42
  (see also Rice cooker)
Rice porridge 48-49
  Cantonese chook 48-49, 52
  Chicken Porridge 58
  Fish Porridge 56
  Minced Meat Rice Porridge 54
  Teochew moi 48-49, 50
  Fried rice 41, 43, 98
    Cantonese Restaurant-Style Fried Rice 45
    Nonya Sambal Fried Rice 46
Rice vermicelli 61, 68, 74
Roast Pork 89, 106

Sago Gula Melaka 158, 163
Salt fish 49, 95, 111, 115

Siew Bak 89, 104, 106
Soups 129-144
  Chicken, Potato and Cabbage Soup 130
  Egg and Glass Vermicelli Soup 132
  Egg Drop Soup 132
  Winter Melon Soup 135
  Wonton Soup 139
Soupy Wonton Mee 141
Soya Bean Cake 93, 117
  Fried Firm Soya Bean Cake with Beansprouts 117
Soya Sauce Belly Pork 89, 93
Soya Sauce Pork Fillet 98
Stringing beans 23
Sweet Potato Soup 158, 167

Tau Eu Bak 89, 93, 95
Teochew moi 48-50
Tofu 93, 117, 118
  Fried Bean Curd with Vegetables 118
  Fried Firm Soya Bean Cake with Beansprouts 117
Tung hoon 12, 27, 38, 61-62, 82, 132
Utensils 10-12

Vegetable dishes 113-127
  Diced Meat and Vegetables 121
  Fried Beancurd with Vegetables 118
  Fried Beansprouts 115
  Fried Cabbage with Crab Meat 124
  Fried Firm Soya Bean Cake with Beansprouts 117
  Fried Luffa with Egg 126
  Min Chee 113, 121
  Vegetable Curry using Curry Powder 153
  Vegetarian Fried Mee 68
  Winter Melon Soup 129, 135
Vegetarian Fried Bee Hoon 68

Weights and Measures 9
Wheat vermicelli 61, 84
Winter Melon Soup 129, 135
Wok hei 63, 79
Wonton, Boiled 137
Wonton, Fried 137
  Fried Wonton with Sweet and Sour Sauce 143
Wonton Soup 129, 139

Yee Foo Mee 61, 63, 76